SLOW DOWN, SHOW UP AND PRAY

Simple shared habits to renew wellbeing in our local communities

Ruth Rice

Authentic

First published 2021 by Authentic Media Limited,
PO Box 6326, Bletchley, Milton Keynes, MK1 9GG.
authenticmedia.co.uk

British Library Cataloguing in Publication Data
A catalogue record for this book is available from the British Library.
ISBN: 978-1-78893-183-0
978-1-78893-184-7 (e-book)

Cover design by Vivian Hansen
Printed and bound by CPI Group (UK) Ltd, Croydon, CR0 4YY

'This book is much like its author . . . practical, inspiring, humorous and hugely relatable. Ruth Rice is not only a great writer, but also a great theologian, a great leader and a great person. Through long and hard work, she has renewed her own wellbeing, moving from a position of languishing, to a place of flourishing. For that I am in awe of her courage, skill and tenacity.'

'*Slow Down, Show Up and Pray* is both inspiring and practical and of course hugely accessible as well. I unreservedly commend it to anyone who wants to help the Church become an even greater expression of Christ among us – a safe, nurturing and welcoming place for all to encounter the grace of God in tangible ways.'

Daniel Whitehead, CEO,
Sanctuary Mental Health Ministries

'Sometimes your own pain, your own unexpected journey to a different (and better) place and the purposes of God entwine together to create something beautiful and worth sharing. This is Ruth's experience as God has birthed Renew Wellbeing [the organization she leads]. This book resonates in my soul, inspires me once again as a church leader on our own journey to connect people with the welcoming love of God and offers huge amounts of practical wisdom that will equip us to travel well.'

Revd Lisa Holmes, Lead Minister of Skipton
Baptist Church, Member of Spring Harvest
Planning Group and the Evangelical Alliance Council

'Ruth has walked her talk, so this book is full of hard-earned wisdom. Not only is it essential reading as we all consider the issues around spiritual and emotional wellbeing, it is also incredibly practical. You will find yourself encouraged but also equipped to think about the wellbeing of yourself and others in new, insightful ways. Highly recommended reading.'

Cathy Madavan, speaker, broadcaster and author

'This is a treasure of a book. It combines an inspiring story of God at work, an invitation to join in that work, and a space to meet with God. It is both deeply prayerful and deeply realistic, both spiritually refreshing and full of practical advice. A must read for those who struggle with their own wellbeing, and those who wonder what churches can do to live better together. A must read.'

The Revd Dr Isabelle Hamley,
Chaplain to the Archbishop of Canterbury

Contents

Acknowledgements   vii

Introduction: Mental Health,
Wellbeing and the Church   1

PART ONE

Connect: The Renew Story   **12**

1. My Story   15
2. The renew37 Story   26
3. The Renew Wellbeing Story   45
4. Wellbeing in a Global Pandemic   55

PART TWO

**Keep Learning: What Makes Renew Wellbeing So
Different?**   **62**

5. What is Wellbeing?   65
6. Be Present   77
7. Be Prayerful   89
8. Be in Partnership   102

PART THREE

Get Active, Take Notice, Give   **116**

9. Get Active: Setting Up a Centre   119

10. Take Notice: Reviewing and Improving   129

11. Give: Multiplying Renew Spaces   134

12. Forging Ahead   137

Conclusion: A Tsunami of Mental Ill
Health, or a Wave of Wellbeing?   145

Appendix 1: Poems and Psalms   151

Appendix 2: Good Practice   163

Appendix 3: Stories from Wellbeing Centres   165

Appendix 4: Great Courses and Resources   179

About the Author   183

Bibliography   185

Notes   187

Acknowledgements

Love and thanks go to all the amazing Renew
Wellbeing family and team
(this is their story, not just mine)
and the equally amazing Rice and Quane family,
to my lovely, long-suffering Mark and fab kids who
have taught me what love looks like and who were
willing to share me,
and the many dear friends who I now consider family.
Can you tell I really value family?
Which is why I long for everyone to know they are
included.
There is only one family, one Father, one great love.
There is only one story and we are all included.

'God places the lonely in families; he sets the pris-
oners free and gives them joy.'

Psalm 68:6 (NLT)

Introduction: Mental Health, Wellbeing and the Church

We walk alone without someone to care . . . but now I have found friends, a new family in a new place! Thank you all! Such a blessing – a safe place in a crazy world . . . wonderful people. Now someone knows my name![1]

I think we all know there is a growing issue with mental and emotional health in our nation and our world. Statistics put it at one in four people who will experience a diagnosable mental health issue in their lifetime.[2] The figure is probably much higher. In many ways it doesn't matter if the figure is one in four or one in 400. There are still people struggling with isolation and mental ill health and that bothers me. That affects me. It affects all of us. All of us struggle at times with some degree of anxiety and stress. Most of us have times in our lives when we feel isolated and alone, even in a crowd or a family. Not all of us have illness, but all of us need wellbeing.

Many of us, me included, know about this first-hand. Some, like me, have failed to spot our need to attend to our wellbeing until it was blindingly obvious and pretty much the only option left to us. Some of us who think we are OK and can't understand mental ill health have a lot to learn from those who know they are not OK and yet have found habits and patterns of wellbeing that are not dependent on being well.

To slow down, show up and pray is going to help us to see wellbeing renewed in our communities. The organization I lead is called Renew Wellbeing. This is not just the name of our small charity helping churches set up spaces like the one I started in Nottingham several years ago. No, I think to renew wellbeing is our first priority, our privilege as humans, a calling both personal and corporate and an urgent imperative for communities and, dare I say, for all churches who claim to care about their communities.

The quote at the start of this introduction is from a lady who I met shortly after we opened our first wellbeing centre in West Bridgford, Nottingham in September 2015. This space was born from my own journey with mental ill health and a need for somewhere to not be OK and yet to be part of an authentic community with an option to practise my faith and inner habits honestly and simply. It was, if you like, a fairly selfish venture. I needed it.

But here was a lady I had lived in the same town as for thirty years, probably passed in the street, saying that she could go all week in our nice, middle-class piece of suburbia, full of churches and cafés, and never hear her name spoken from one end of the week to the other, except when it was attached to medical notes and a label of mentally unwell. Her simple statement was that she liked our café, our renew space (which had taken her weeks, by the way, to be brave enough to get through the doors of), and that in this space she was now known and named and not alone. This simple statement stopped me in my tracks. Whatever I thought I was doing opening renew37 for myself, however busy we had become serving our community as a church, God had his ear turned to people like this lady who we had not seen or heard in our cosy churches and over-full programmes. How could there be people on my patch, where I had lived and served as a Christian leader for years, who went unnamed, who were so isolated and for whom simply having people who knew their name was all they wanted?

It floored me. It still does. There are still people we are labelling and not naming. But surely there is a mental health system to help people like this? Surely this is not the church's job? We are increasingly aware that the mental health system is oversubscribed and people are falling through the gaps in care, despite the good efforts of dedicated staff.

This is not an issue the church can ignore. Indeed, we are not ignoring it. We are helping, serving . . . very often at a loss to know how to help others and be honest about ourselves. We are all involved in mental health. We all have mental health. We all need to look after our wellbeing.

The phrase 'It's OK not to be OK'[3] is being used widely now in 'mental health speak' and I would suggest that the whole heart of what Jesus taught and the church believes is held in that small phrase. I think the language of wellbeing could possibly be our common language that allows us to hear each other as humans again across the many divides we have put up over years. This may be the best time ever for churches to become really engaged in their communities again.

But what response is possible from a church made up of humans who are also not really OK (well, at least some of us aren't)?

What can we realistically and sustainably offer to help our communities to improve their mental and emotional wellbeing? What can we actually *do* about it? And, who are we called to *be* in a world full of people like us who are not really OK?

If you, like me, are troubled by how many people are struggling to attend to their wellbeing, how many of our young people are suffering with depression and anxiety and how often the church feels like the last place people are looking for answers to this, then this book might help you know your own story, live your own habits and create spaces for others to join you.

I'm no expert in mental health. I am an ordinary Christian with an ordinary story, but something extraordinary seems to be happening around me. Since the opening of our first renew space or wellbeing café in September 2015, we have seen God call other churches to join in this revolution of ordinary showing up: presence, prayerfulness and partnership.

In the last two years we have grown from four to fifty centres nationally, run by every denomination and sometimes by beautiful ecumenical partnerships that seem to be working. But this is an invitation to a story that's really only just started. It's an invitation that comes on the back of a global pandemic which has shocked the whole world and claimed many lives. Now we know: none of us are OK. It's an invitation to prioritize wellbeing at a time when the message of hope needs to be lived out on every street.

This book is written as a resource to help you consider your response and your church's response to the growing crisis in mental and emotional health. This book is an invitation not to do more but to do less.

To slow down. To show up. To pray.

To be human. Together.

From the moment I slowed down, showed up and admitted I was not OK, from the moment I invited God to fill my emptiness and asked the church to help me be more honest, look after my wellbeing more and learn how to be fully present to God in a way others could join in . . . something simple and beautiful began to grow around me.

In Mark 4:26–29 Jesus tells the parable of the farmer who went out and planted seeds:

> And he said, 'The kingdom of God is as if a man should scatter seed on the ground. He sleeps and rises night and day, and the seed sprouts and grows; he knows not how. The earth produces by itself, first the blade, then the ear, then the full grain in the ear. But when the grain is ripe, at once he puts in the sickle, because the harvest has come.

This little story has come to mean such a lot to me as the little seeds of Renew Wellbeing planted in broken ground have sprouted. As I have slept and woken, prayed and played, attending to my own wellbeing, something I have not seen before is growing, and it looks a bit like God's kingdom. And I have no real idea how something so simple is growing so much!

We will be using the Five Ways to Wellbeing[4] as a template. These five suggestions are from a nationally recognized piece of research into what people found helped them with their wellbeing, real habits you can actually engage in: connecting, learning, getting active, taking notice and giving.

When I first heard about these ways to wellbeing from my friend Rachel in mental health services, I was excited to realize that the church has been engaging with these ways to wellbeing for years. Often, though, our inner and outer habits around these five ways have been hidden away in little house groups and church buildings that are not accessible to the very people who are needing them.

I suggest it is time to open up the box and find ways to get our very real habits of wellbeing around these five ways out in the open, where we can share them . . . and maybe even remind ourselves to slow down and take another look at them as churches. Maybe churches could become groups of people showing what wellbeing looks like and living differently at the heart of every community. This could be a shared language. There is a real willingness for dialogue right now between faith communities and statutory services; the door is wide open to find new ways to improve access to help and support in the community. This is a good time to be part of a community group like a church and to take a long, hard look at how to open up what is so good about the local church to those who think that 'no one knows their name'.

There has never been a better time to think about what wellbeing actually is and what it looks like in practice. I believe this is the whole gospel, the good news we carry, that it is genuinely OK not to be OK. And that God has a church he is getting ready for just 'such a time as this'.[5]

Do you want to join him in turning a tide, a tsunami of mental ill health into a wave of wellbeing? Here's one small story and a few ideas of how to join in.

I will invite you first to *connect* with the Renew Wellbeing story, so that you can decide if it might be part of God's story in your life and therefore help you connect more deeply with your own wellbeing and the wellbeing of your community.

Then I will take you through a *learning* process with the three principles of a renew centre:

Be present
Be prayerful
Be in partnership

. . . looking at the basis for these three principles and how they are working out in practice in our centres.

Finally, I will use the last three ways to wellbeing *get active*, *take notice* and *give* to provide you with the tools to try out these ways to wellbeing and principles in your own life and to introduce them to your church and your community: getting active in setting up a centre, taking notice as you attend to rhythms of prayer, reviewing and sharing what you are learning with the rest of the Renew family as it grows. Then there is an invitation to give away what you are learning so that we begin to see a web of wellbeing across a nation.

In many ways, I can't teach you to do what we are doing. I can only share a story and some values and principles, and then the space you set up will be the teacher; in actual fact, God himself will teach you *through* the space.

This Renew Wellbeing journey is one way to join our learning together, to share, to improve, to grow as we see wellbeing renewed on our piece of earth.

Before you begin, take a moment of stillness to remember this is not about you doing more. There is a God. It isn't you and it isn't me. What a relief. He is renewing wellbeing. Maybe we can join in.

Over the years I have been a Christian I have read so many books, many good, but nearly all made me feel I should be doing more, being more. Many contributed to my burnout, I'm afraid. I pray that this will not be just another one of those books. This is a call to do less, to simplicity, to stillness, to a way of being, not a flurry of doing.

This could be an invitation to you to live more deeply in your own story of brokenness and wellbeing and therefore to live the beautiful gospel more freely with those around you.

PART ONE

Connect

Keep Learning

Get Active

Take Notice

Give

Connect: The Renew Story

I get some relaxation time for myself socializing with other people who care and understand. It has given me somewhere to go on a regular basis and to make new friends and meet old ones. I am allowed to be who I am. If I'm low I feel better when I have been. Life becomes a better place and it gives my carer a breather.[1]

Connecting: When I heard this way to wellbeing explained, it was a simple invitation to anyone struggling with mental and emotional health to try to make a connection with another person or group.

This seems impossible when you don't feel great. It's not as easy as it sounds. Connecting when you feel disconnected is not that simple. I began to wonder when I wasn't well if there was a deeper level of connecting needed. Not just connecting to another person but a connection with oneself and a deeper connection with the God who made and loves us. All connection can be helpful, but I believe that finding this is at the heart of all wellbeing.

I invite you to apply this simple way to wellbeing, to *connect*, as I tell you my very ordinary story and our extraordinary renew story which will give you some space to reflect on your place in God's bigger wellbeing story.

1

My Story

I couldn't love you any more and I will never love you any less.[1]

Burnout

When I first lost my voice, it was really amusing to everyone. I think my family thought all their Christmases had come at once: 'Speak up, Mum.'

At the time I was a wife, a mum, a church leader and a full-time primary school teacher, and was living the dream. Yes, I had bad days, but mostly I knew I had lots to be thankful for – a loving husband, three great kids; I had a long-held and strong faith in God and a church that was good to be part of, where I could use my preaching gifts, and a job in a great school doing what I loved: teaching. In my spare time I loved putting on pantomimes and shows at school and had a motto that 'every child had a right to a standing ovation'. I had been brought up in a loving Christian home and had supportive family around. My hobby was talking!

My father-in-law had once said my mouth ulcers must have been caused by friction, I talked so much. So, to find myself unable to speak for a week was funny.

I carried on teaching, of course – with a tambourine to get the children's attention and the help of a good teaching assistant. I prided myself in not having a day off. After all, busyness is next to godliness, isn't it?

But as the weeks wore on and the eventual time off school with the accompanying fatigue came, it began to feel less funny.

Chronic bouts of laryngitis with fatigue were the physical symptoms, but under the surface a deeper dark time had set in.

I remember standing in the kitchen and feeling it was all too much, and sliding down the wall, big tears rolling down my cheeks. I spent long hours in my bed. My parents came to stay to help look after the kids. Mark, my husband, got on with being Mum and Dad. I could hear this all going on but as I had no voice, no energy and no desire to leave my bed, I had to let the world go on without me.

It made me cry knowing I was letting my family down, my school down and myself down as a Christian . . . surely I was not meant to feel like this. Friends would want to visit but I asked Mark to keep them at bay. I didn't know how to explain what I was feeling even if I had had a voice.

I now recognize the voice loss, fatigue and depression as symptoms of burnout, but I kept the mental and emotional symptoms well away from public consumption. Surely proper Christians didn't get depressed?

Don't pat me, I'm not a dog!

Worse than not being able to work or see my friends or care properly for my family was the going to church thing. Up to this point church was part of the answer, even though I suppose the busyness around church activities may have contributed to my burnout. Now, however, my rare visits to church were excruciating. Everyone was lovely. They were worried about me. There were lots of hugs and lots of patting and stroking. Many people wanted to pray with me and every time they did, I felt this extreme pressure to be well, to get my voice back, to get my energy back and to get on with my life. It made me panic. I knew I couldn't go back to my life yet . . . I couldn't cope with it. I didn't want my voice back. The whole praying thing felt like a huge pressure where I was going to get found out.

Eventually my dear friend made me a sign 'Don't pat me, I'm not a dog!' and the patting died down a bit, but mostly because I rarely went to church and if I did, I went late and left early so I didn't have to face people. I couldn't sing the songs, but I did love to be in the place of worship. I knew I needed God's presence, but I so didn't want all the baggage that went with the church experience.

I realized how many other people must feel like this when for all the right reasons we do all the wrong things and make church feel like an unsafe place to be when you are not OK.

Not a spatula
My return to health was slow and had many twists and turns. A miraculous healing at a New Wine[2] conference was followed by another bout of voice loss and ill health when I failed to make any changes to my lifestyle on recovery.

I journaled all the way through my illness when I felt able to. I'm so glad I did. As I read those journals I now see that time of low mood, depression, voice loss, burnout and fatigue was one of the richest in my life. I did not enjoy it one bit. I wish I had never gone through it, but in it I met with God in a profound way.

Once I realized life went on without me and God wasn't 'using' me, like some sort of spiritual spatula, I began to understand that he loved me anyway.

There weren't many beautiful moments, which is why this one I am about to describe has stuck in my mind for so long.

I was lying in my bed unable to get up, I felt so low. Suddenly I felt that God was right next to me and he whispered, 'Ruth, I couldn't love you any more and I will never love you any less.' I was doing nothing! I wasn't earning his love. I wasn't serving anyone. He was just pleased to be spending time with me. I wrote in my journal: 'I would rather not get my voice back and have this intimacy with you, Lord, than go back to being like I was before.'

This was the beginning of a change. I began to stop expecting to be able to pull myself together and took the doctors' advice more. He had said I had depleted my deposit and current accounts emotionally and if I was to recover, I should save up any energy in my deposit account, not spend it in doing too much.

Peace, pace, place

I began to explore and practise peaceful habits. Meditation on the Bible, quiet prayer, mindful walking and many other simple practices were completely new to me and I realized I had been missing out due to over-busyness. I needed peace and to maintain it I needed peaceful daily habits. I began a love affair with the Psalms that lasts to this day. A daily habit began of reading a psalm, choosing a phrase and meditating on it; choosing to dwell only on those words and chew them over and over in my mind and heart instead of going over and over my worries. The Psalms gave me permission for prayer to be whatever I needed to say to God, positive or negative, praise or lament. The Psalms became like rooms my soul could make itself at home in and I began to find expression for my own deeper longings and losses.

Slowing down the pace of not just my life and activity but also my thoughts and worries was key. Peaceful habits brought me into a healthier pace of life. I also found that specific places can be really important for good peaceful habits, and being beside still water really helped me. I knew that walking by water brought me peace, so would try to take a daily walk when I felt able to and sit by a lake, a canal or a river. The sea is even better, of course, but living in landlocked Nottingham I still found some lovely places to reflect and rest. I visited various retreat centres where I discovered beautiful quiet habits of meditation and prayer that I began to incorporate into my new pace.

Holding the cup

Holding a cup helped. It helped me to reconnect body, mind and spirit, something I had not really known how to do. Holding my first cup of tea in the morning in both hands, I used that image to remind me that I am held in the safe hands of God and that he still loves me. I re-engaged with a brilliant book that my great friend had given me, *The Cup of Our Life* by Joyce Rupp.[3] I have to admit that when I had first received this book, which takes the reader on a six-week journey of inner life habits, I had been less than impressed. I had always been of the opinion that life is too short for this sort of 'navel gazing', as I called it. I had been scathing of the 'wasted time' spent not doing kingdom work.

But as they say, 'desperate times' . . . So I picked up this amazing book and started to properly engage with breath prayer (a way of praying that acknowledges breath as a gift and that uses fewer words, a type of meditation), Lectio Divina (the spiritual reading of the Word of God: slower, more repetitive) and stillness (the hardest of all).

As I began to be able to connect with the world around me again I was able to hold the cup, meditate on the Psalms and breathe, maybe more deeply than I had ever done.

This simple habit of first cuppa breath prayer then enabled me to get up and start my day with a 'resting thought rate' (the 'go to' thing you are thinking about when your mind is at rest) that was more peaceful and less anxious. I realized that it was anxiety and a sense of being overwhelmed that had made me take to my bed in the first place, so replacing my great skill of worrying with a simple practice of meditating seemed to be helping.

Breathing in and out slowly with a couple of words from a psalm, picturing the cup of my life emptying of clutter and filling with truth – this became my simple daily habit. I would then bring myself back to the cup and the breath prayer every time my mind began to spin or my thoughts began to overwhelm me. I would take the habit on my walk and with my footsteps I would repeat the simple truth of the meditation to myself. 'You, Lord, are my Shepherd' or 'the Lord is my stronghold'. Whatever the psalm phrase I had chosen that day, it had to be always good and always true for me, not a mantra or a self-confidence trick, not mind control but simply filling my mind and heart, my walking and waking moments, with something good and true to get my mental teeth into.

And breathe!
I had learned so many wonderful things growing up in a loving Christian family and church, but there were *so* many that it felt like a pressure to try to 'have a quiet time', or study, or work through a prayer list. This practice of a simple phrase and breathing was all I could manage but seemed more profound to me than anything I had

engaged with in the past. It began to dawn on me that 'less is more' can apply to our thought processes and overactivity too.

My internal dialogue has always been so dominant, so controlling. I was almost at the mercy of any thought process going on in there. I suppose I felt it was my duty to get it sorted in my head and to then sort everybody, serve everybody, live the truth correctly once I had got it in my head correctly. I had previously been unaware of the constancy of the internal chatter but during my illness, with only myself to talk to, I became aware of the voice and the presence of God, the ugliness of my own self-deprecating banter and the beautiful whisper of God , as I had never heard or known him before.

My conviction was beginning to grow that in order to really engage with others, to really serve others, to receive from others, we first need to engage with God, with ourselves, with the empty cup of our lives.

Solitude v loneliness

I remember recently listening to Radio 4 in the car as they discussed the subject of loneliness and the need for community. You would think I would love this. But I found myself shouting at the radio as person after person gave definitions of the opposite of loneliness that involved someone else meeting our needs. It had begun to settle in me that the opposite of loneliness for me was an acceptance of solitude. Until I had learned to be alone with myself and the God who loved me, I was always going to need someone else or something else to fill the void. I was addicted, if you like, to people – helping them, fixing them, being helped by them.

Don't get me wrong, I am not now saying that we don't need each other or that everyone needs to become a hermit, but I suppose I had realized the hard way that in order to approach another human authentically and honestly, without needing them to be something for me, I had to be at peace with myself, at home with myself.

The lens

I read during this time some life-changing words in a little book called *Life Together*[4] by Dietrich Bonhoeffer. This man of God had been a German pastor and theologian working and writing during the Second World War and involved in the Resistance. His observations around what constituted good community were all the more stark for the setting in which he was writing. He suggests that we must never approach another except through the lens of Christ, and more than that, he states that any attempt to control or get what we need from the other puts us in the place of God who is the only creator of community.

I remember being offended by this the first time I read it. I had spent so much of my life 'being Jesus' to people – or so I thought. I had believed that if I didn't show them God's love, they would never know it. I had felt it my responsibility to try to help anyone in need, and my duty to be the one who was there for people who needed me.

It was this very preoccupation with my own importance in the story of other people's lives that had led me to the inactive, sorry state I was now in. I am not suggesting for a moment all mental ill health is self-inflicted, but mine certainly had elements of self-righteous self-harm in it.

As I read Bonhoeffer's words over and over and sat them alongside Jesus words in Matthew 11:28–30, 'Come to me, all who are weary . . . and I will give you rest',[5] the light came on. I had spent so long wanting to get it right, to be needed, to be useful. I had wanted to serve God and others, but in doing so I had failed to realize my own humanity, my own need, my own brokenness. Bonhoeffer's idea that we need to approach any other human only through the lens of Jesus Christ was a shocker! Of course, only God himself would be the one who really knew me and my motives, and really knew the others and their need, so why would I simply offer myself when I could offer him? It was obvious as I re-flected that any other approach had me trying to make others fulfil *my* needs, even if that was my need to be needed by them! It was subtle but it was shocking how very different this approach felt.

As a leader I had cast vision and wanted people to be-come all I thought they should be. Who was I to do that? I was not the creator of community. I was a partic-ipant in it. God created community. God is community. Three in one.

Recovery . . . a wandering, not a sprint

This dawning realization of my own part in the big story was key to my recovery. I was loved, I was unique, I was gifted. I loved people, but there was a God and it wasn't me. If I stopped, the world would still spin on its axis, and to love others from any need of my own would always leave me wanting, would always lead me to control or trying to fix.

Only as I meditated on the truth of my being held, his unconditional love, my total dependence on him, his choosing of me just for the sake of being with me . . . this began to warm my soul and heal my over-busy heart.

I spent my empty days walking and sleeping and resting and recovering, and the panic seeped out of my bones.

2

The renew37 Story

Turning the sound back on

By the time God had healed my voice – a miracle, and an overnight one at that – I was ready to listen to him and make the necessary changes, going part-time at school, training in missional leadership and eventually giving up teaching to serve as pastor at New Life Baptist Church, West Bridgford, Nottingham. This was the very church who had loved me back to health despite my irritation with all the patting.

The church was brave in choosing me to lead them as their pastor because they knew I could break. There was no pretending I was superwoman, no hiding.

This was a healthier way to start than it felt. No masks, but a much deeper understanding as a church of what so many people were going through. And a real compassion to do something different.

Returning to serve in leading the church, I knew that part of my call was to those who felt like I had – only worse and for longer. Some of my friends in the church had suffered with mental ill health for many years; some were unable to continue working and were facing long empty days. My short journey into darkness had made me more aware of how difficult it must be to live with long-term mental ill health, and how the church can be a good family for those folk, but can also feel unsafe, too jolly, and can put undue pressure on people to be well again when they are unable to control how they feel.

The unsung heroes
When I was waiting in the church car park for the welcome to die down so I could safely sneak in, over those long dark months, I met other shadow people. Those I had not noticed when I was in the thick of it. Amazing, faithful, brave sorts who refused to give up their church family even though the pain of the weekly event took every ounce of their courage. Those who were determined to keep showing up even if their heart was quivering inside. Those who risked misunderstanding and overhandling in prayer every week, just so that they would be in the right place when the lights came back on. These heroes I learned to listen to and love. These often overlooked ones, or sometimes patronized ones, had understood something about the gospel that I had never known.

I began to spend more time with those who knew they were not OK than those who didn't know yet – meditating together on the Psalms; not trying to answer each other's questions, and finding different questions even to replace the 'How are you?' or 'Are you OK now?' ones that were unanswerable honestly in the time allotted.

One such friend had had so many dark days, so many suicide attempts, such difficult things to deal with in her life. After being on a mental health section in hospital for several years, she returned home to a care package of just a few hours' a week support. It was not enough and we tried our best to support her, but I found myself constantly worrying about her and often running her to A & E, as the local council mental health services crisis team were often too busy to deal with her. I sat in case reviews pleading for more support, complaining bitterly about the advice and help she was receiving, ringing for professional crisis support, to be asked whether or not she had stroked her guinea pigs, which was one of her activities from her therapy that did sometimes help but seemed ridiculous when her cry of despair was so deep.

People of peace in council offices

I began to realize that there was no other help to be offered. The system was giving all it could. I met amazing professionals during these days working in mental health services. I don't believe anyone went into these services to do a bad job. The stress of the workload was getting to everyone. I met good, kind people, devastated that they had had to leave folk on long waiting lists.

I met an amazing local councillor. I had gone to complain about care in the community, and when I had finished my rant she said, 'You are right, Ruth. Let's pray!' God has his people everywhere. It took the wind out of my righteous complaint! As we bowed our heads and prayed right there in the council office, I knew God was in this with me.

The ideas I had for a renew space flowed during that conversation, and soon this dear lady was introducing me to people of peace who are still in my life, valued friends and advisors to this day. I met Michele, called to leave psychiatry and train for the ministry, who brought her years of experience to being one of my greatest encouragers and advisors. I met the fabulous Rachel, who became a firm friend and advisor and who, from her place in the council mental health team, was able to work with us as we asked different questions about how the church could be healthily involved more. She was a co-producer in the purest form in making renew37 happen. So, as well as keeping pressure on government to increase funding, we began to pray about how we could better support the folk in our church with mental health issues.

Coming out from behind closed doors

I had begun sharing my habits of meditating on the Psalms with some of my friends and had got good feedback about how helpful this was. A group started in a friend's house and we called it the 'Cup Group'. We simply sat with our cups of tea and meditated together on a psalm, sharing only how easy or hard we had found the habit, learning a new skill together. It became popular and went from one group, to two, to three.

There was a hunger out there among people of faith and no faith to practise habits that would deepen our inner lives.

People who were struggling with long-term loss or undergoing cancer treatment found these shared times of quiet, these simple universities of ordinary habits, particularly helpful. Our groups were often full of folk who would struggle with Sunday church, but were desperate to be with others who believed and to pray. However, these weekly hours at my house and other homes were not enough. People had long, empty days to cope alone with what they were carrying.

Many of those struggling with inner darkness would never come into our homes, however welcoming they were. These were still closed clubs for the initiated. My heart was still towards the ones no one could see, behind closed doors, desperately lonely, struggling with the darkness that I had found unbearable even though I had a church and a great family.

How could we be there for these? How could we slow down and show up, make prayer available where anyone could access the rhythms and learn from one another?

As I got more and more involved in the lives of those struggling away in the mental health care system, with large gaps of time between helpful therapies and nowhere to go, I realized I was again trying to be the answer, to personally meet the need, and I couldn't do that. I was aware that it would be easy to be overwhelmed with need and my health would suffer again. I needed to attend to my hobbies and prayer rhythms. I needed to remember to see people through the lens of Jesus, to sit with them in his presence and let him do the work. But where could I do that and how could it happen? Where could I paint my stones, crochet, create and look after my inner health, with others? Where could I pray my prayers and breathe in his presence, not just on my own, but together and available to anyone, in or out of the church? How could I look after myself and invite others into that?

The 500-mile big think

Well, the story continues with a 500-mile round trip in 2014 a couple of years after I had come back to a degree of better mental health and had begun leading the church.

My first 500-mile round trip to Ffald-y-Brenin, a Christian retreat house in Pembrokeshire, was a journey of discovery for me in more ways than one. I had read about the amazing things God was doing in this quiet place of natural beauty, and as I was in need of some healing after a bouncy castle injury had left me with neck and back problems (for church leaders, a note of caution: don't use a bouncy castle as a illustrative tool for a sermon, as the point of the talk gets rather lost when you are 'back-boarded' away in an ambulance). I was more than a bit sceptical about places being in any way special. I headed off for a day visit. This was a 500-mile round trip from Nottingham.

It was more than just a quest for personal healing though. As a church (New Life Baptist Church, where I had begun to be full-time pastor and had attended since it was established) we were talking about premises. We had been a church without a building for all of our life together and although at times this was a blessing, we had begun hankering after somewhere to call home.

I was very keen to see what a 'house of prayer' looked like, as I had found some great personal practices in the contemplative movement during my time of burnout. As a charismatic church, it seemed to me that prayer would be a good focus for our 'place', if we ever got one. The thoughts and plans were no more formed than that.

As I journeyed to Ffald-y-Brenin that February day, I could not have imagined the longer journey that God was about to take us on as a church; a journey alongside friends with mental and emotional ill health; a journey that would see us partnering with a local business and the local council; a journey that would take us to a little café, not a big meeting hall . . . a journey into new habits and activities that turned our church inside out and saw the beginnings of a national movement.

I received more than healing that day; the healing was fantastic, don't get me wrong. I sat in the little prayer chapel in silence, I joined a small group of total strangers in simple read prayers and psalms, and I knew that there are indeed 'thin places' between heaven and earth where the air is thick with the felt presence of a God who loves us and comes close to us and heals us.

As I drove the other half of the 500-mile big think, the feelings of joy and amazement began to be replaced with feelings of frustration and annoyance.

A strange response to a good day out, you might think —
here is some of my inner dialogue that day: 'That was
amazing . . . M could do with coming here. Oh and C, oh
and P and C would love it . . . the peace of it.'

All these dear friends in the church were struggling with
mental ill health and often I felt the way we did church
didn't help. Big meetings, noise, a pressure to feel the
joy! I knew what I had just experienced in quiet places
would be just the ticket for these good mates.

'Maybe I could bring everyone here. I wonder when and
how we could do that? Hang on! Why am I thinking of
bringing everyone on a 500-mile round trip when what
I have just experienced was down to the Holy Spirit and
surely he is everywhere — even Nottingham?'

I began to wonder where there might be houses of prayer
in Nottingham. I made a mental note to look it up when I
got home. Then more thoughts began to crowd in.

'Wait a minute, what am I thinking? Surely wherever
"two or three are gathered" you are there "in the
midst",[1] and New Life has more than two or three people. What on earth are we doing every time we gather,
if we are not experiencing his presence and power and
love like they are at Ffald-y-Brenin? Does God love Wales
more? Surely he would like to show up like that all over
Britain . . . all over the world?'

I began to mentally shoehorn the practices of silence and
liturgy and slow singing and reading into our existing busy

timetable of churchiness. I began to plan and scheme for how I could get people to come to prayer together.

But hang on, I thought: the people who really need the sort of healing and presence and love that come from places like this are never going to come to something too churchy, too 'Christiany'. What about my friends who are often saying how stressed they are? What about my neighbours who would never come near a church meeting but do seem to want to know You? How are they ever going to have a Ffald-y-Brenin moment?

Irritation at the church and its structures began to take over the tune in my head. I replayed old messages I often heard internally about exclusivity and Sunday gatherings. What had started as a lovely day out for me turned into a full-scale rant by the time I got home.

Needless to say, with this sort of loving attitude to church, the next few months were not plain sailing. No one got a Ffald-y-Brenin experience as we lurched from one property to the next in search of somewhere to land as a church. My constant refrain about prayer being important somehow led to the whole leadership team taking the 500-mile round trip in the November of that same year, 2014. I was limping inside by then, after one too many defeats in the elusive search for a property to have church in. It's often hard to find the answers if you are asking the wrong questions!

Our experience this time over several days together was rich and unhurried. I received a good patch-up of my inner wounds and the team 'got it', whatever 'it' was.

One team member said the ground was shaking the whole time she was there. We decided on our return to shelve plans to find a property to meet in and just look for somewhere to get praying together. We were hooked. We knew a rhythm of daily prayer was the only way forward – forward into what, we were less sure about. We had tried daily prayer tucked away in a kindly lent barn conversion, and although the few of us who made it had met with God there, it was not the accessible available space I had dreamed of being able to get praying in.

We also agreed that whatever place we met in had to be inclusive of all and accessible to all, particularly those who felt marginalized and isolated. Our heart was still for those who were struggling with the balance of their minds, and we pondered how to share our own habits of wellbeing as we all owned the struggle of being human.

Having agreed to stop pushing God for a big place to have meetings and start serving the most vulnerable, including ourselves, we didn't have to wait long. A few weeks after returning, God had given me a powerful dream about opening 'renew centres', and as I asked him what they were and we continued to pray, the approach came from a local business to share premises.

People of peace at Tiffin Tea House

Jo and Diane, the wonderful owners of Tiffin Tea House, my local favourite place for a coffee and cake, approached me during this time.

'You're a minister aren't you, Ruth?' they said. Not sure what gave it away! They began to share their concern for folk who were coming in each day on their own and how lonely they were. They asked if I could chat to people, as they did not have time to run the business and have as many conversations as they wished. They had lovely ideas for shared tables with 'crafty' activities.

I was delighted. An unofficial chaplain to a lovely café with great cake! Someone had to do it! But it was not as easy as you might think. I don't know if you have ever tried working out who is lonely and who wants to be left alone, but it was not long before I became a kind of social stalker.

We began to think of other ways to give people choices. If they wanted company, how could we have a space they could opt in to, and how easy would it be to do that?

Out of these discussions came the possibility of taking on the lease of the space next door to the tea house. After much discussion and legal wrangling (two different landlords, a charity and a business, a new adventure for church and community), we were able to knock through between the two places and draw up an agreement to share the premises. Monday to Thursdays the two places would be separate but with similar décor and ethos; one side a regular business, the other a place that looked like a café but felt more like a shared front room. A place where everyone knew who you were, where you could stay all day if you wished. A place where you could belong. Friday to Sunday, Tiffin Tea House opened through and had full use of the double space to expand their business. The rent was shared.

New Life Baptist Church was quite simply amazing during this shift in focus. We had so many plans in our heads for a building that looked like church, where we could have all our meetings and services. To take on this expensive lease meant giving up all those plans and continuing the rent of a school on a Sunday. It meant the congregation digging deep for a little place that most of those who paid for it would never use. It meant reimagining church as a small quiet space for those who were not part of church. And New Life went for it! A 100 per cent positive vote for this 'out of the box' idea amazed and thrilled me. As a leader, there are moments when it's not hard to love the flock.

Hilarious provision
Over the summer of 2015 the church worked hard and dug deep, and every last penny of the significant amount of money needed for the renovations and rent agreements came out of their pockets from God's hand. Not once did we tell them how much it would cost (it was eye-watering) and on the last day of August, before opening the doors at the beginning of September, every

last penny, to the penny, had come in. It was nothing short of miraculous and it rewrote the church's rulebook on how God provides and on his hilarious generosity for this church.

It had been a long hard slog, but during it we had begun to pray together in the room that was to become the renew space at 37 Abbey Road, morning, noon and end of day. We had to work around the builders but the priority of prayer was set first. The peace of God even on a building site was tangible and the priority of prayer was established. Under the first layer of paint we wrote all the words, scriptures and promises God had given us. We planned what activities we could bring to our shared front room.

We put in walls to create a lovely little prayer room attached to the café-style space. The 'quiet room' was big enough to seat about fifteen in a simple circle. It was here, in the space where the prayer would take place, that we prayed even before the walls went up. We knew from our visits to retreat centres that a dedicated prayer room was absolutely essential, and there were some discussions about doors that folded back to make the room multifunctional. Bear in mind, the church had no other building than this little rented space. We met in a school hall. Understandably, some folk were excited about having a space to do all sorts of meetings and clubs. But we felt as a team the purpose of this space was clear – prayer and a welcome for the most anxious and isolated. I felt we needed to keep one space special and was delighted when one of our leaders had a picture from God of Jesus standing in the quiet space and saying, 'Just for prayer . . . this space is just for prayer.' The church agreed. When I think back to those meetings, the sense of being of one heart and mind as the church tried to understand the need for a place of wellbeing, I am in awe of God's work through the obedient people of New Life Baptist Church and am so grateful to them for taking so many risks with me.

We invited the whole church to think and pray about what part they could play, and most did think about it. It was with a small team of those who really got it that we started in September 2015 for a trial run for a few weeks. It felt anti-climactic, to be honest; after months of hard work we just showed up, prayed and put the kettle on. People took a long time to trust we weren't going to get 'churchy' on them; those who felt vulnerable took even longer. We often just sat, two or three of us, happily crafting or restoring furniture or knitting, wandering off to the prayer room and being still and wondering whether we had heard God right. But day in, day out the peace of the place seeped into our souls and drew people in. Four years on and the place was still opening four days a week and was full of people needing a place to belong.

Redefining experts

God had sent people to be alongside me in this who were not OK themselves, and they became the experts, the most listened to, the ones who knew how hard it would be to get through the doors should it became too full, too jolly, too fussy. One dear friend who went on to open our second centre would 'police' the set-up every morning and I would take careful note of how the space affected her mood.

She would tell me in no uncertain terms when we had it too full of stuff. She would spend long amounts of time in the prayer space, proving how essential it was to have the quiet room set up next to and accessible to the social space. She, and others like her, really were the founders of renew37. They were the ones who stopped it becoming yet another busy project serving the 'poor people'.

The authenticity, the peace, the fact that it needed to be a space we wanted to hang out in and be creative and inclusive in, was key. Working on a welcome that was not over-the-top but allowed each to come and to bring their gift, not their label, was a steep learning curve. It still is. We are so much more comfortable when we can segregate and label and divide with a service counter or a bag of help. To sit together and be equal: now, that is hard. That requires us to see ourselves as human, to recognize our own vulnerability and to work hard at listening and being present to each other and ourselves.

renew37 launch
At the end of September 2015, we officially launched renew37, the first 'quiet shared space where it's OK not to be OK'. *Renew* because we longed to see our own and other people's mental and emotional health made new, to see community renewed, to see hope renewed and

37 because it was 37 Abbey Road, and Psalm 37 talks about not fretting so much. Simple. We were asking God to renew that little patch of earth; number 37. We loved it from the start and are loving the adventure of helping others open such simple spaces of wellbeing as one space began to become many spaces.

You see, it was obvious to us, as it is to others who have now joined the family, that one place was never going to be enough, that a place on every street to share would be more like it! And so the story moved to phase two: Renew Wellbeing.

A virtual tour

It's hard to understand, until you have seen it, what the difference is between a renew space and a regular café, even a Christian one. So I will take you on a virtual tour.

The street, Abbey Road, is very much like any suburban shopping street. As you approach you see Tiffin Tea House. It looks very much like an ordinary pretty café. Except on closer inspection you see it is joined to the shop next door that looks very similar but has the sign 'Renew37' over the door. It looks like a café, there are people sitting around drinking coffee in both sides. But in renew37 there is something different going on. It is run by a local church, New Life Baptist Church. It is a wellbeing café, and as such doesn't sell anything!

It is a place to come and attend to your wellbeing by joining in activities or sharing a hobby. The kettle is always on, or great cakes and coffees are being brought through from the teashop next door. Jigsaws, knitting, colouring, chatting . . . friendly faces but a quiet buzz. It seems calm. Then just as lunchtime approaches, the person hosting the space invites everyone to leave what they are doing if they wish and join in a prayer time. Even people who are not churchgoers seem happy with this.

The prayer room is right next to the café. A simple calm space with seating round the edges and a cross on the wall. At different times in the day someone invites people to relax and sit quietly in God's presence. A simple pattern of someone saying a line from the Lord's Prayer and others praying simple short prayers, or just saying one word of a country or person they want to pray for, follows. It's all very calming and no one feels obliged to pray out loud. There's a short reading from a Gospel and a blessing, and then people quietly go back to the café, which is any faith and none, or go home. It's strangely simple and wonderfully calming.

Then later a member of the mental health team arrives and others join her and you realize this is about mental health and wellbeing, and no one is embarrassed to talk about what they are struggling with and no labels have been applied. No one has asked for your referral; you are welcome to express any views with respect for others.

The group talk about a bike ride and discuss the next week's group. They leave a few hours later, content to have made some new friends and had a chance to get some advice.

Then others arrive, young people and older, a wheelchair-user starts putting up shelves and a young man begins drawing. Quiet chatting over activities seems to have everyone engaging.

As the day draws to a close again, there is the invitation to the quiet room. Some folk are already in there, just sitting quietly. One person is sitting in front of a light box a friend has brought in for him to try. Another is writing a poem, a psalm of his own to help with his loss.

The quiet is lovely and we are asked to rewind our day and look for signs of love and beauty. People begin to say thank you to God for simple things . . . sunshine, a smile, a nice cake.

Then we are asked to think of the things that have not been lovely and beautiful. This causes some frowns, but as we remember the news and how it troubled us, the person we met that we couldn't help, the way we avoided that person we don't like, it is a relief to be encouraged to accept forgiveness and to put down anything we are carrying that is not ours to carry.

As we accept the blessing for our dreams to be good and our sleep to be peaceful, it feels like a great way to end the day. This really is a café where somebody knows your name and you are welcomed as you are.

Quotes from regulars

Helping open up and set up has given me a chance to make friends with people I wouldn't have got to know. I have learned a lot about being present. I have learned the value of not rushing around and being busy all the time.

I have met friendly people at 37 who have helped me cope with my depression and have lifted my mood. I feel I have learned a lot from the different people here and I will keep and cherish the experiences I have had.

I have really enjoyed coming to 37. The people are lovely! It is light and sunny. You don't have to join in the activities unless you want to. I really look forward to it after the weekend.

I like meeting people . . . having a chat and perhaps a laugh. It's very relaxing and non-threatening.

I like that because of the friendships I have made at 37, Sunday morning church feels like family. The quiet space is a good sanctuary if it all gets a bit much.

It's great to come and pray and chill out with people you wouldn't normally see. The mental health group has opened my eyes to people's stories. It's been really good to come every Monday and not just get on with jobs on my own.

There is maturity about mental health at 37. Good to have access to occupational therapy in a relaxed setting.

3

The Renew Wellbeing Story

*I like that there is always something to do while
you are chatting. I like how much everybody cares
about you, whether they know you or not.*[1]

A web of wellbeing across a nation

Within a year of opening renew37 it was fairly obvious
that something was going on here that was so good, so
simple, so life-giving to church and community that it began to attract the attention of other churches who had
recognized an issue with mental and emotional health.
We began to get a steady stream of visitors from other
churches to renew37, joining in the prayer rhythms,
marvelling at the simplicity, asking about how to partner
with mental health services.

Another local church began to plan how they might open
a space using an existing café rather than renting their
own place. Other churches began to ask if they could use
their church buildings. A church in Doncaster who had
been sensing the call to establish a shared space on the

high street came to visit to see if a renew space might be for them. All of these wonderful churches had the same heart and had heard the same call. But all of them needed my attention and help, it seemed. I began to try to work out how to free up some time to be available to others without wearing myself out again by also continuing to lead the local church full-time.

Into the Dragon's Den

At this point, Cinnamon Network,[2] who help Christian social action projects multiply, were beginning a venture where they invited new projects to pitch for an amount of seed funding at a *Dragon's Den*[3]-style event in London, where various funders gathered to hear innovative social action ideas and choose one to give a significant sum of money to as a start-up. After much soul-searching, knowing that to win the money would mean stepping back from church-based leadership (and I loved my job), I applied. We won half the money, which was amazing but not quite enough to give up the day job. It meant being able to step back from leading church two days a week to make myself available to the other churches wanting to set something up.

The other wonderful part of the win was the input received from the Cinnamon Network team about how to replicate. Here was a whole new language and concept, way beyond anything I'd learned. I had completed a Master's degree in missional leadership in preparation for leading church with 'For Mission' which was life-changing and foundational for what was to come.

But the learning that I received with Cinnamon Network was really helpful, thinking about how to help others to do what we had done at renew37. Over the course of the next year we were able to assist several of the churches to start renew centres.

But I was aware that the call of God on my life was to plant renew centres in the land.

The Deborah dream

I'd had a dream a few years previously while on the '7 Deadly Sins of Women in Leadership' course (based on the brilliant book of the same name by Kate Coleman[4]). The dream had come whilst considering one of the deadly sins, which according to Kate is not having a clear enough personal vision.

Whilst on the course I had been reading about Deborah in Judges 4. In this chapter it explains the situation in the land at the time. It was a desperate time of darkness and difficulty and oppression. Deborah was sitting between Bethel, that is, the house of God, and Ramah, that is, the place of weeping. From that place she could see what needed to be done. This seemed really significant. A place to sit between two worlds was what I had been feeling was needed for the church in the mental health crisis. I began to think about a place we could sit between the world of meetings and church services and the pain and despair around us. Having described the situation in this passage, which was desperate (very much like the desperate state of the mental health situation I was seeing around me), it says in verse 4: 'Now Deborah, a prophetess, the wife of Lappidoth, was judging Israel at that time.' Deborah then goes on to help the nation be set free from oppression.

I have always loved the story. Deborah is the sort of woman I wouldn't mind being like. I must have been thinking about this story as I went to sleep. In my dreams I could see a desperate situation on my own street. As I looked at perfectly lovely houses, I could see behind those closed doors to the depression within. And from behind many closed doors there was a thin cry of despair.

In my dream I could see down the streets and around the whole town. It was like a Google Earth moment. The more I could see, the more I could hear that things were not OK. That even though it looked like people had everything they needed there was despair, depression and isolation behind many closed doors.

As I woke up, I heard these words:

> Now Ruth, wife of Mark, a missional leader, was planting renew centres in the land at that time.

I quickly wrote down these words. It felt like maybe God had spoken.

I suppose what I needed to know was what on earth a renew centre was!

So you see, it wasn't a complete surprise when renew37 was not enough, that it was renew centres plural, places of peace and not just one place for one church that was on God's heart.

I can't say that I often hear from God like this; I suppose that's why it is stuck in my mind and I believe it to be a mandate from heaven.

From Cinnamon security to real risk

So after winning the Cinnamon Network money to get started helping other churches, it was never going to get any smaller when the money ran out.

And a year later it did run out. It was either go back to church-based leadership with one renew centre and carry on helping one or two local churches, or be obedient to God and take the plunge – giving up the day job to really see renew centres multiply.

I took a few months' sabbatical in September 2016 to explore what it might look like to lead local church part-time and set up a charity. God spoke to me constantly about giving up the church-based leading and trusting him, but I returned to local church ministry in the December 2016 convinced I could have a go at doing both. At the Fresh Streams conference[5] in January 2017, as was often the case at this amazing gathering of mission-focused leaders, God really turned up the volume. I left that few days away under no illusions about the call of God to leave

New Life Baptist Church as their leader with its safety and lovely bunch of supportive folk to lead and its very generous stipend. God had almost audibly spoken and confirmed through his Word and the testimony of several others that the time was right to step out in faith and trust God to provide. In case I wasn't listening, as I waited at the door of the conference centre, a lady I had never seen before approached and gave me £5,000 to 'start my charity'. Unprompted, by me at least, this was the final confirmation.

Leaving New Life took a long time. Mark, my husband, and I eventually left in July 2017 to start the charity Renew Wellbeing.

These were our dear family and we still miss them terribly. But God was true to his Word and provided trustees, a wonderful team, churches that were interested in setting up renew spaces and every penny needed to get started in miraculous ways.

He is still providing. We are completely dependent on him. Once Renew Wellbeing was constituted and accepted as a charity (of which renew37 was now just one of its centres), we were able to respond to the interest of other churches, receive visitors to renew37, and offer training and speaking at other churches interested in renewing wellbeing.

The Renew family grows
Over the next two years we saw the number of centres rise from two to nearly forty. Many churches were

contacting us to come and speak, share, train and encourage them as they also wanted to be present, prayerful and in partnership for the wellbeing of their community.

Appendix 3 holds the stories from around the UK at the time of writing as told in the words of those amazing hosts of other centres and details of how to get in touch with these centres are on our website (www.renewwellbeing.co.uk). These are the real heroes. These are churches that are turning up week in, week out. I love these stories. We are careful not to tell stories of individuals. These are not ours to tell, and as there is no pressure to be OK, we are not measuring success by improved wellbeing, but simply by the willingness to keep showing up.

God had a lot of work to do with me about what I thought a renew centre was. I was so sure it needed the church to leave the building and go on the high street. I was so keen that everybody opened something like we had. God had to show me there were many ways to set up a renew café.

Replicating *not* duplicating
Some renew spaces like renew34 in Hucknall, Nottinghamshire, use their existing building to very good effect. One of the most successful centres at replicating is St Giles' Wellbeing Café in Northampton, which is held in a large old Anglican church building once a week. This is neither a beautiful café space nor a constant presence,

but it is working. It is being present, being prayerful and being in partnership. It most certainly is renewing well-being in Northampton. It has to date replicated itself six times in local churches.

One of the first replications for renew37 was in Ruddington village near to West Bridgford in an existing café space run by a person of peace who was happy to host the church to set up a weekly renew space in her café. None of this felt ideal. There was a prayer corner and not a prayer room, and the ability to make sure the whole space was a place of peace was more difficult.

However, God was showing me that this is his work done his way and that he loves his church. He is more than happy to start with what we have in our hands.

The latest addition to the Renew family as I write is in Northallerton in Yorkshire. Here, five churches have worked together, becoming a charity themselves to set up a place on the high street called the Living Rooms where the downstairs is given over to Renew 5, a quiet shared space that looks like a stunning shared front room with kitchen and prayer space. Upstairs there are rooms for counselling, services and more direct intervention that can be signposted. The whole community has got behind this project. It has taken a long time to get off the ground but deep roots could well mean great fruit.

It is so exciting when someone takes a cutting from the little plant you put in the ground and plants it way deeper in their soil in this way. The beauty of being a Renew family means that the learning from this centre becomes available to all of us. The bar has just got higher for community co-production and church unity.

In the Isle of Man, where my own story began back in 1965, it is beautiful to see three renew spaces so far. Two of these are being run by another charity, Drop Inn Ministries, who can bring churches together to open, non-threatening spaces in towns and villages. The other is repurposing an existing café next door to the church building which is a simpler way to use the space than trying to run a business, which is what many church cafés become. I can see a web of wellbeing on the island spread easily into all the little unused chapels and forgotten villages where good people of faith live.

In Purley, London, the Churches Together group that invited me to speak to them have started with one renew space in the Baptist church but are running it together with a view to rolling it out across the other churches. A beautiful co-working vision.

In several of our spaces – for example, in Chipping Camden, Gloucestershire, and Worcester – it is already becoming clear that to be exporters of wellbeing into surrounding villages and isolated communities could well be part of God's plan.

Often the approach is coming from a person of peace in the community. In Powick, in Worcestershire, there is an amazing team running a therapeutic horticulture project who approached the local churches to set up a renew space in the middle of the nurseries once a week. They even built a prayer summerhouse right in the middle of a working garden centre. It's beautiful. When churches are brave enough to leave their buildings and find out where God is already at work, there are people of peace like these folk willing to co-produce.

I was reminded of the feeding of the 5,000[6] where the miracle of replication happens with five loaves and two fish because that was all they had. I am beginning to understand that God is very happy to start with what we have got in our hands, even if it doesn't feel like very much.

For many churches, they are rich in resources but have overpromised and are overworking. This call to slow down and show up is not just for the community but is also, I believe, God's compassionate call to his frazzled church.

So, let's take a look at what makes a renew space different from all the other amazing social action and café spaces that churches are already running. Why would you want to join in this story when you are already engaged with your community, already serving in lots of ways? Why has this particular way of being church taken off so quickly? What's the attraction? What are the principles? But before that . . . who could have foreseen that since I began writing this book, we have faced a global pandemic that has emptied our church buildings and also has caused us all to reflect more deeply on wellbeing?

4

Wellbeing in a Global Pandemic

How to renew wellbeing when all the renew spaces are shut

In February 2020 with fifty-three renew centres open nationally and twenty more churches in preparation stages, we celebrated together at our annual AGM and commissioned new team members to help with the rapid spread of this simple movement.

No one could have been prepared for the fact that just a few short weeks later the world would be gripped by a global pandemic and nothing would ever be the same again. All fifty-three centres closed overnight. Hundreds of already isolated and anxious people who had been finding hope, community and belonging in our centres were plunged into the same awful world of daily briefings, fear and isolation.

It was a grim day when I sent out the message to all hosts to close their cafés and centres. Churches were quite rightly concerned that they needed to be present as they had promised. But there was no other way and little or no time to prepare for it by setting up new systems and gathering contact details.

Some churches had good technical support and could quite quickly make spaces available online via Zoom etc. Others rapidly set up WhatsApp and Facebook groups for the regulars they had contact with. For most, the situation was less cut and dried. We had encouraged churches to have a relaxed approach, no need for gathering names, addresses or phone numbers and no referrals. Therefore there was no personal information held and stored on regulars visiting our spaces, and this made it really hard to keep connections in lockdown.

It's been so sad to hear of regulars struggling with their mental health and the increased isolation, not able to access community due to limited technology at home. But it's also been humbling to see church after church connecting with us week in, week out to discuss how to move our renew spaces online and keep being present, prayerful and in partnership. We know it's not ideal. We know many cannot cope with this way of connecting, but it's better than nothing, and there are some amazing stories of hope emerging as we settle into long months of social distancing.

We quickly drew up guidelines for churches, made homespun videos, set up Zoom discussion groups for leaders and hosts, and declared every Wednesday a wellbeing Wednesday to pray together for the *shalom* of the nations. And then we realized that renewing wellbeing was exactly what was now needed, and would be essential for churches coming out the other side of this global crisis.

The church, flung out of its box of meetings and services, may never make it back in. We may find new ways to be present in the communities we have come to know in a much closer, more neighbourly way during this awful time.

Our prayer at Renew Wellbeing is that we learn as God's people in lockdown how to *be* church, not *go* to church. That we become more present to God, ourselves and others. That we learn to pray like never before and make prayer our native tongue again. That we find ways to make our habits of wellbeing available to those around us reeling from the shock of these months. And that we learn to not just applaud the NHS and key workers, but to stand alongside them in kingdom work, particularly in mental health services.

Our prayer is that the new sense of vulnerability, the need to be honest and lament will bring a deeper listening in our churches and communities to those who already knew they were not OK – the experts in the room. Those with lived experience of mental ill health can now teach us a thing or two about dealing with anxiety and stress, about navigating loss and living with unchangeable difficulties.

The new training manual on our website for what we began to call 'Renew Communities' still looked at the three principles:

Be present: Of course, this was the trickiest thing . . . no social contact meant using Zoom and other online platforms, having a phone line, a Facebook page and sending things out on the post; each church doing what they could manage, not what everyone else was doing. This had always been our advice: use what you have in your hands. So for some churches, sending out little packs with craft activities and prayer cards was what they felt able to do. For others, they opened a daily Zoom room for folk to pop in with a hobby, bring a cuppa, starting and ending with prayer for those wishing to join in.

It has been heartening to see that those churches who had taken the leap and begun to slow down, show up and pray knew where the isolated folk were; they had taken time to be there for them. They had also set aside time and developed hobbies and prayerful habits that helped sustain them. God had been preparing us.

Be prayerful: This has become even more important – the one thing that not even a global pandemic can stop. Churches have increasingly been engaging with rhythms of prayer to help have a sense of connection as they pause and pray together. Many churches asked for our prayer materials, and we have been so heartened with how many have realized how very key prayer is. We have been helping churches work out how to keep shared prayer times using technology, and then how to make those times accessible to anyone. People wanted to pray before; they *really* do now. It is our privilege to share our prayer habits. Let's make sure we prioritize this.

Be in partnership: This has been really hard for our churches who had been building good links with community mental health professionals and feel they have to start again in many areas, as our services struggle to work out how to access all their isolating folk in the community. Some councils realized early on the need to partner with community groups, and have mobilized the resources of existing Renew hosts and connections. But for many, the use of Zoom as a platform is making it hard to connect with councils who are rightly concerned about using a public platform to discuss mental health issues and have issues about security and the internet. New partnerships are emerging, though, as we stand together in our localities and see kindness, the best of humanity and the caring side of a usually over-busy world. We can build on this in our future partnering.

After lockdown

I am writing this a few weeks into lockdown and we are beginning to offer online training now to any church wanting to use this time to prepare to open spaces when lockdown ends. There will be a massive need for connection, for safe places, for prayerful spaces. The church will need to remain slowed down, to keep showing up and pray.

It is interesting how even in lockdown we can become over-busy in our church leadership agenda, with a 'fix it' mentality of a million Zoom meetings. I believe the slow, steady habits of wellbeing and peace will be what the bride of Christ can offer to a broken world and will need for its own honest recovery.

We will need to plan for using spaces not our own – parks, open spaces, allotments – as continued social distancing may make some of our buildings difficult to use. Maybe we will find better ways to be present in the green spaces of God's good earth.

There are many unknowns, but what we do know is that there has never been a better time for churches to get stuck in to their communities with a real, honest offer of simple habits and a rhythm of wellbeing and prayer that they are engaging in themselves. There really is no 'them and us'. None of us are OK really. We all need to attend to our wellbeing. The power dynamic of the church being able to offer to fix people cannot exist in the realm of mental and emotional health. There is no 'bag of wellbeing' to give out. We have to live this slowly, steadily and prophetically.

God is still very present. His hands still hold our empty cups. People will be seeking him. How can we make it simpler for all, however anxious and isolated, to find his peace?

PART TWO

Connect

Keep Learning

Get Active

Take Notice

Give

Keep Learning: What Makes Renew Wellbeing So Different?

Be present
Be prayerful
Be in partnership

Keep Learning: This way to wellbeing refers to the fact that is can be good for your mental and emotional health to learn a new skill, fact or hobby. It may seem that renew spaces are very much like all the other amazing things churches are doing in their communities: coffee mornings, drop-in centres etc. So what makes Renew Wellbeing so different? Why would a church want to engage with this charity?

We have made our learning into a simple set of principles so that any church can safely get involved in mental and emotional wellbeing. It is time to share learning across the church as we face this wellbeing challenge.

Our renew centres have many and varied opportunities to learn from each other. The 'bring a hobby, share a hobby' mantra of our cafés is simple but effective in allowing all to be both learners and teachers. But this way to wellbeing also applies to the way we run the whole charity. We co-produce: that is, we produce things together. We choose to learn from our partners in mental health services, from those with lived experience of mental ill health, from our mistakes and experiments. We keep in touch so we can keep learning from each other. We review regularly and retrain annually. The learning is also deep inner learning about who we are and who God is. This sort of learning never ends and can really improve wellbeing. But I am realizing that the deepest learning is about wellbeing itself and what relationship that has to the gospel.

Learning to attend to your own wellbeing and learning how to share your wellbeing habits with others is a lifetime's adventure, but I believe it starts with a few simple principles: being present, being prayerful and being in partnership.

5

What is Wellbeing?

Defining terms

Mental wellbeing describes your mental state – how you are feeling and how well you can cope with day-to-day life.[1]

Before we look at what makes a renew space unique, let's define our terms. We won't be able to know if we are renewing wellbeing if we aren't sure what wellbeing is.

The independent collaborating centre What Works Wellbeing? takes its definition from work done by the Office of National Statistics. It says:

Wellbeing, put simply, is about 'how we are doing' as individuals, communities and as a nation and how sustainable this is for the future.[2]

Martin Seligman from the positive psychology movement, in his book *Authentic Happiness*[3] talks a lot about our strengths being key for our wellbeing.

What is your definition of wellbeing?

Take a moment to consider this question.

For me there are two key words and one key image that help me understand:

   Shalom
   Dwellbeing
   The cup image

Shalom

This Hebrew word translated 'peace' in the Bible deserves further study. Hebrew is a rich language and a one-word translation never quite gets to the root of what is being taught.

I believe the word 'wellbeing' is a better translation than 'peace' of the biblical word *shalom*.[4]

Shalom has three root shapes in the Hebrew, and looking at other words with these same root shapes we see words which mean:

   Shelem: paid for
   Shulam: fully paid

It therefore is closest to complete peace, something that is wished as a greeting on arriving and leaving, a desire for complete wellbeing. It means complete, paid for, paid in full, whole, more than peace – wellbeing!

Shalom has an altogether deeper meaning and draws us to understand that we can have wellbeing even when all things are not equal and we are not well. Wellbeing as *shalom* is promised to all, and to all creation, by God. In Isaiah 65:17–25 we see a prophetic vision of what this *shalom* will look like. In Christ this *shalom* is brought near to all. In Matthew 5:3–11, Jesus declares blessing over the broken, the mourning, the meek and the persecuted. This word 'blessed' is more than just wishing them a bit of happiness, it is the Greek word *makarios*, the highest form of wellbeing known to humanity, spoken over dead dignitaries, over kings and princes. Here, shockingly, Jesus is declaring that wellbeing or blessing over the least in society. The kingdom is near. Jesus opens up the possibility of peace, *shalom*, wellbeing to all. Therefore this cannot mean *shalom*, peace or wellbeing is only available to those who get their act together, try harder, or have their emotional and mental seesaw in balance.

It is so hard to describe wellbeing and that is why there are so few decent definitions out there. I feel we have to 'live' wellbeing, to be a human experiment in wellbeing, to be prophetic communities of *shalom*, showing what is possible by trying it.

I had wanted to write a kind of wellbeing thesaurus, as I have been so concerned about the unhelpful way language can be used to label or isolate people.

It seems that these simple renew spaces are a kind of living thesaurus. The amount of times people have come to visit a renew space after hearing me speak about it, and I have heard them say: 'Oh, is that all you meant? I get this!' It is almost too simple for words to be adequate. But simplicity is not easy, or cheap, or quick.

Shalom, real *shalom* at the core of all creation, is a work of a lifetime, of eternity for God, and therefore in our own lives and community it is less a commodity to be won and more a lifestyle to be lived together.

Dwellbeing

Dwelling implies remaining, staying, not rushing. This is something I have had to learn about the hard way. One of my favourite chapters in the Gospels is Luke 10. Imagine with me following Jesus with these disciples who were ordinary folk like us. Ordinariness was the thing Jesus looked for in who he called. Gives me great hope!

So at the start of this chapter we see Jesus sending out the disciples with instructions to take nothing with them, to take the hospitality of others and to stay there bringing the gospel with blessing. This is the 'being in partnership' part of the principles of Renew Wellbeing:

Be present
Be prayerful
Be in partnership

Somehow we have complicated this to: 'Let's try to get people to come to us and get them into church, giving them what we have.'

So you can see in Luke 10 the disciples rejoicing that they get what their calling is, to share the gospel and change the world.

Jesus then tells them a story, the parable of the good Samaritan. And they add to their understanding of world-changing the need to care for those in need, for social action.

We as a church get this too, and loads of amazing social action is happening across the nation.

But then, just as the disciples think they've got their activities, world-changing message and mission sorted out, Jesus throws a curve ball and takes them with him to Mary and Martha's place:

> Now as they went on their way, Jesus entered a village. And a woman named Martha welcomed him into her house. And she had a sister called Mary, who sat at the Lord's feet and listened to his teaching. But Martha was distracted with much serving. And she went up to him and said, 'Lord, do you not care that my sister has left me to serve alone? Tell her then to help me.' But the Lord answered her, 'Martha, Martha, you are anxious and troubled about many things, but one thing is necessary. Mary has chosen the good portion, which will not be taken away from her.'
>
> *(Luke 10:38–42)*

What? They had just understood the call of God and Martha seems to be fulfilling it by serving and getting active, and Jesus states a preference for just sitting! When I read this, I, like those disciples, was feeling for poor Martha. What about you?

But the 'good portion' was to sit at the feet of Jesus and be with him. It still is. Being present. Being prayerful.

If we become so busy serving him that we forget to look at him, love him, listen to him, simply be with him, we miss the whole point and can put our own name into the lament of Jesus: 'Martha, Martha you are anxious and troubled about many things, but one thing is necessary.'

For me it took the period of ill health, not as bad as many of you have been through, not given by God, as he is the giver of good gifts, but self-inflicted burnout, for me to realize *one thing* was necessary and work out what that *one thing* was.

Psalm 27:4 tells us the one thing the psalmist wanted. Not a bad place to start:

> One thing have I asked of the LORD, that will I seek after:
> that I may dwell in the house of the LORD all the days of my life,
> to gaze upon the beauty of the LORD and to enquire in his temple.

Dwelling, gazing, enquiring.

One thing.

Dwelling. Us as his dwelling place.

But what does that look like? What are the habits? Here is one image I have found helpful . . .

The cup

When asked what I understand by wellbeing, I hold a cup half-full in both hands and ask, 'Is the cup half-full or half-empty?' I get various answers but give my answer as: 'Both.' There is always joy and always sorrow in the cup of our lives.[5] Then I draw attention to the hands around the cup and say, 'For me, wellbeing is knowing who has got my cup; knowing I am held regardless of circumstances in a much greater love, a bigger story. Wellbeing consists of habits that help me keep my eyes on the hands around my cup, habits that help me, a chronic worrier and control freak, to stay in 'the peace of God, which surpasses all understanding, [which] will guard your hearts and [our] minds in Christ Jesus' (Phil. 4:7).

Dwelling in him and he in me is a lifetime experiment in 'the practice of the presence of God' which was so well expounded by Brother Lawrence.[6]

As I have said, I often explain wellbeing for me as the image of the cup empty or full, held in God's hands. I often speak of the time when I was ill as 'cup emptying' and the habits I learned as 'cup filling' and then warn of the danger of using my cup to fill others instead of going to the source.

I use the image of immersing the cup into the jug of water from which I have been filling it. I call this 'dwellbeing'. God dwells in me and I dwell in him. I want to make my life a 'practice of the presence of God', immersing myself in him all the time. Me in him, him dwelling in me. That is, until that day in Wimbledon when the very attentive listener in the front row asked after the service, 'I know what the cup is – that's me. And I know what the water is – that's God. But what's the jug?'

Mmm, good question! I mumbled some stuff about the whole world being full of God and it being hard to fill an entire room with water to make my point. We laughed, but the quizzical look was still there. I knew I hadn't answered the question well.

What is the jug? What am I immersing myself in when I talk about the practices I have and share, and when I ask churches to consider shared habits of dwelling in his presence? Is the renew prayer space the jug? Do we have to have a prayer space to do this – is wellbeing only available to those who have enough time to join in with a community practising shared habits?

That can't be it. God is fair and good. His gifts are available to each. So, how is wellbeing experienced by you and others around you? How can we see it renewed, or at least improved? Psalm 72:19 tells us that the 'whole earth [is] filled with his glory', so in one sense the jug is everywhere; the whole world – nature – we can meet him and practise his presence anywhere.

The church is also his dwelling place. We read in Ephesians 2:22 that we 'are being built together into a dwelling place for God'. Together, as we learn to live and forgive and give, he dwells. We can't know the fullness of his dwelling all on our own all the time. Prayer is not just a personal thing, it is a corporate thing. He dwells in the glue that holds us together, in the shared air we breathe.

You are also made in his image. I can see him in you. Whoever you are. He made you on purpose and the more I spend time with those who know and admit they are broken, the more beauty I see. But I am his dwelling place too. Me! That's always the toughest one to swallow, right? In my skin, that's the skin he is in. He wants to sit with me and walk with me and cook tea with me and watch Netflix with me.

So, the jug is not just the beautiful prayer room at renew37 or any other prayer space; it is my every breath. But I do believe a space can act as a reminder, a prophetic image, as it were, of what it is like to be immersed in the presence of God, where it is not one person as carrier and the other as receiver, but where we are all 'infected' with his presence, his grace, his love. Finding these spaces, creating these spaces, was key to the idea of a renew centre.

The early understanding came not just with the visit to various retreat centres that were such 'thin' places between heaven and earth, but also meeting God powerfully at coastlines and on mountains and knowing it must be possible to tune in to this ever-present God of peace literally anywhere.

Once, I had called a prayer time for our church folk at the borrowed barn conversion we used frequently. As is often the pastor's lonely lot, I was there by myself. Even prayerful churches find gathering for prayer meetings hard. And if I am honest, that day, I was disappointed. It was shortly after the first encounter at Ffald-y-Brenin and way before renew37 and I had hoped if I called the church to pray with me every day, we would see the amazing things happen with us that were happening in Pembrokeshire. I was after something!

So, that day when I prayed alone in a cold empty room, I was disappointed. I closed my eyes and ranted at God until the ranting ceased and I began to practise meditating on my psalm phrase that day. I don't know how long I sat there, but as I prayed for the sake of his presence, not prayed for things and miracles, just prayed like breathing – enjoying his presence – the atmosphere changed, warmed and I felt as if the room was filling up with his Spirit like a swimming pool filling with water. I felt I would need to learn to breathe differently or drown.

It was then I opened my eyes and realized the whole room had filled, while I sat there, with God's people. One by one they had crept in and joined the silence and this collective silence was powerful, beautiful. This was what I had dreamed of for our town, my neighbours, our community. This was the heartbeat a renew centre needed.

Not just lonely inner practices, but a shared life of prayer and peace.

Places of prayer; places of presence; places of partnership.

So armed with these three words and pictures – *shalom*, dwellbeing and the cup – let's take a closer look at the three Renew principles. Basically, if these three are in place we believe it is a renew space. But without any one of these three we risk burning ourselves out, and we ask you not to put the Renew Wellbeing label on it.

If we engage with the issue of mental and emotional health simply by showing up and being present, how will we sustain this when there are things we can't handle or fix and when the triggers to our own mental wellbeing are challenged? What do we offer when there is no 'bag of wellbeing' to hand over the counter?

If we just pray, there is no doubt God will do amazing things, but how will people know they can pray too? Could we make prayer into one more area of dependency on the other, where we pray for and not with others? Could it become just a private club for the initiated?

If we fail to partner with existing services, who will we signpost when we know we are out of our depth? Or will we try to fix people, pray for them in ways that are more helpful to us than them, over offer and give without boundaries?

Be present . . . but with a co-produced ethos. No 'them and us'. Names, not labels. Not the church giving and others receiving, not a power dynamic to fix problem people, but a strength-based approach of sharing what we bring.

Be prayerful . . . where this means shared quiet space and habits, made simple enough for all to join in. Not praying *for* but *with*. A constant place of God's constant presence open to all.

Be in partnership . . . not just a signposting arrangement, not just a way for services to find good community groups to refer people into and socially prescribe, but a real working relationship, proper co-production, where voluntary group and statutory authority bring something to the table and co-produce a more sustainable way of community working.

Presence + Prayer + Partnership = potential for renewed wellbeing.

6

Be Present

Slow down and show up

The first principle of renewing wellbeing for yourself and your community is being present. By this I mean really showing up, not just being on a rota for a programme, or popping in for a few minutes, or even being there physically. Being present requires a full engagement with the present moment, the people who are around you, your own emotions and even a recognition of the presence of God himself. This requires the slowing down and showing up referred to in the title of this book.

For me, the simple act of giving myself fully to the present moment was a contributory factor in my return to health. For many, the pandemic we are presently going through has afforded us time to be at home more and rediscover hobbies and simple pastimes. We have slowed down, but have we showed up? Have we truly noticed the moment we are living in and those around us? So often we are physically present but mentally and emotionally stuck in the past or the future. I used to rush through tasks and even meetings with friends, thinking of all the things I hadn't done yet. Even enjoyable moments became an item on my to-do list.

For each of us personally, this being present is simple but very hard. Having a hobby that engages your whole being, having a conversation in which you are truly listening, having your whole self engaged in a simple daily task; these are ways to meet with the God of wellbeing; these are ways to show up in your own life.

To take these everyday habits that are very personal and share them can be a very powerful thing to do in a society that is self-orientated. It is powerful to have a space that is shared by anyone wanting to practise the art of being present; the simple fact of life that this moment is the only one we are guaranteed.

There are some basic values that we have learned and are learning together as a Renew family that help to sustain the simplicity of being present. These values can apply to an individual journey of wellbeing, too, but here we will look at how the local church can adopt simple practices to make wellbeing flourish in their communities.

Values
A strength-based approach using the Five Ways to Wellbeing
To maintain presence for wellbeing we have found it to be really important not to approach people as problems to be fixed. We are being present in our renew spaces

in a way that says each person is a gift from God and unique. We all have gifts and talents and strengths. A long journey with mental ill health can bring you to a place where all you can see is your problem. In renew spaces, we seek to draw out people's strengths, to remind them that they are God's masterpiece. Ephesians 2:10 says 'we are [God's] workmanship' or, as the New Living Translation puts it, 'we are God's masterpiece'.

When I was unwell, I became unable to see any good things in my life. I could only cry out to be made well and forgot there were loads of things I was good at and enjoyed. Each person coming through the doors of a renew space carries strengths and interests, and the aim is to help each one to engage again with themselves and others, in hobbies and interests that bring them life. This does not ignore the things that feel broken, but acknowledges that we are not defined by that one thing.

In our renew spaces we have had people teach us how to restore furniture, make planters, grow vegetables, make bird boxes, speak another language, do origami and much more. This reflects the creativity of the God who made us. People have commented on how refreshing it is to come to a place where no one is measuring whether you are better yet. If the assumption is that none of us are OK really but that we all have gifts, then we don't need to keep measuring or keep waiting until we are 'better' to engage with what is good about us.

The analogy of the cup has again been helpful to me in this regard. I often call this the 'cappuccino life'.

A cappuccino is a mix of bitter coffee, frothy milk and chocolate on the top. It is not just one thing, and neither are our lives. There is always a mix. In with the sorrow there is joy. In with the struggle there is creativity. Along with the need for treatment for illness, mental or physical, there are still things we can do and enjoy.

I had a sense that I would be useless until I was not mentally and emotionally broken, but I began to understand that engaging fully in what I could manage, being fully present even in my brokenness, brought peace and wellbeing even when I was not being well.

Our centres are simply spaces where all can come and attend to their strengths, whatever stage they're at in their wellbeing journeys, without pressure to achieve or recover.

As I thought about what this might look like, I came across the Five Ways to Wellbeing through my engagement with the Nottinghamshire County Council co-production team. I was thrilled to discover the language of wellbeing these offered, and the way the church could engage with them.

The New Economics Foundation has developed a set of five evidence-based actions for a major new government report into wellbeing that, if practised regularly, can improve personal wellbeing. These five ways are being talked about widely by health and wellbeing agencies.[1]

They therefore provide a framework for churches to engage with their communities and with health professionals.

I believe they can be a simple shared language not just about outer habits, but also about inner values.

For the purpose of understanding the values of Renew Wellbeing, we will take these five ways one at a time and use them to explore what makes this very simple way of getting involved in mental and emotional health, work. (Even though we have already looked at how connecting works, here I am looking at each way to wellbeing again so that their value can be understood at a personal level too.)

Connect: This first way to wellbeing is at the heart of all that is done in our renew spaces. For each of us personally we need connection with others to stay well and we also need to connect with ourselves and ultimately with God. Connecting with the world around us, with nature, is also good for us as humans. It is how we are created to thrive. When I was unwell, I became disconnected from others due to my own shame and from God due to a lack of habits of stillness. Finding ways to make good connections with our own emotions, with others around us and with God is nothing new. But having spaces where this is a key aim can be new for churches who quite often get so busy running services and meetings that to simply connect and to be present in the connecting can take second place. In a renew space the connection with others is important but we also give space to connect with God and with the bigger story of our lives.

Keep learning: Learning new skills and hobbies has been shown to be good for wellbeing. In our renew spaces we don't simply show up and sit in circles hoping a decent conversation will happen. We show up to learn. We have hobbies and activities at every table. Everyone is encouraged to bring a hobby and a spare to share. In this way we can all learn and we can all teach. The continued learning is not just in the activities available, but also in the way we set up and run our spaces. When we set up renew37 in September 2015, it was in a continued learning relationship with council mental health services, those in the church with lived experience of mental health issues and others in the community with a heart to see a space to share skills. We build in to each space a review process so we can keep learning. The only way to really learn is to be prepared to fail. This sort of learning requires the team to be truly present, to listen to those around them, to be prepared in the moment to change things, to show up in the learning process. I have learned all I know about mental health issues and challenges by asking my friends questions over lots of time spent together and by truly wanting to partner with those who know and understand more.

Get active: In our renew spaces we might look like we are sitting around drinking tea and colouring-in at times, but each space is encouraged to get active in many ways. This goes beyond simply doing exercise, although we know this holistic view is really good. We are body, mind and spirit and should not compartmentalize these. I found this out the hard way by not listening to my body and allowing my mind to run ragged with worrying thoughts. Each renew space has indoor activities to activate the mind, and many have outdoor activities if there are enough hosts to facilitate this. Coming out of lockdown we are encouraging churches to use any out-door spaces, such as gardens, parks and allotments, so that social distancing can be observed. But even before this pandemic, there were many unused green spaces around our church buildings and cafés that can be put to good use in a renew-style simple way. Some do gar-dening, some plant up boxes with greenery, some go on bike rides and walks (although this needs to be at each person's own risk and additional to the steady presence in the space). We can also get active in our inner lives by actually practising the habits of prayer and meditation, not just talking about them.

Take notice: In its raw form, this way to wellbeing is en-couraging us to practise mindfulness, about which much has been written. In our renew spaces we encourage every activity to be done thoughtfully and the 'being present' value means that we are always taking notice. In our prayer rooms we encourage all to take notice of their breathing, their posture, the world around us, what is troubling us and then to take notice of a sense of the presence of God. Often when I talk to churches, they ask most questions about this way to wellbeing. We have spent so long concentrating on doing over being that to really take notice of every moment can be a hard skill to master, and we need each other's help to do it. When we set up the first space, I can remember finding it so hard to settle to one task, to just sit at a table and do one activity. I had to be constantly reminded by good friends that the space was for me too and to take notice of the discomfort but to stick with the activity in hand. In this way I began to learn to notice the little things to be thankful for and not wander off and try to be useful.

Give: This way to wellbeing was the most surprising one for me when I first saw this list. It was what made me think that these five ways would be a great language for the church engaging in wellbeing. But I also realized that so often the church was not giving people the opportunity to give. So often when we spot someone with a need we want to try to help. We begin to make that person a project, and soon they have no chance to be able to give, which would be good for their wellbeing. As a church we had always been those who gave to others, and so we should be. But in the area of mental and emotional health, there is no bag of wellbeing to give away; there is only the opportunity to create spaces where we can all give and receive our own habits and lives. In this way, we offer all a chance to give. In our spaces, all are encouraged to make their own drinks if possible, to serve each other, to contribute, to bring a hobby, to teach others. The church team are also attendees. We use the language of hosts and regulars, not volunteers and service users. We have to learn how to receive to allow others the dignity of giving.

So these Five Ways to Wellbeing are key to our learning. I love to apply them to my own life personally, so even if you decide not to set up a renew space to practise these five ways together, these can be a useful list to help you ask yourself better questions about your own wellbeing. I run through the list when I feel down and often realize I have stopped connecting in some way, or have not learned anything new for ages. Often I have been inactive and have begun to worry, which takes the attention away from taking notice properly. Sometimes I see that in an effort to protect myself I have stopped giving, or more often, I am giving too much in an effort to run away from being honest. Quite often it is not that I need to do more of any of the five ways, but I spot where I am doing too much in one area and slow down. A five ways audit of the heart can really help reset habits that have slipped or stop us doing too much.

I fully believe the local church has been practising these five ways for centuries and if this is what is needed for the wellbeing of our communities, then it's time to take the walls off our habits and share them in simple spaces.

No 'them and us' and 'names, not labels'
As well as being a strength-based approach using the five ways to wellbeing, we place a big value on these two simple phrases: no 'them and us' and 'names, not labels'.

These are linked, and in some ways are just two different expressions of the same value. All are equal when it comes to mental and emotional health. As I have said before here, none of us are OK really. Some of us are medically unwell in our mental and emotional health, but many others experience, or will experience, loss, anxiety, despair, low mood, depressive thoughts. I am not minimizing real mental health conditions that need proper medical treatment. But I am saying that to some degree, all of us need to attend to our wellbeing and none of us are the experts except in our own wellbeing. No two people are alike.

For a church to run a renew space, there needs to be an acknowledgement of the fact that we will not be able to fix anyone, even ourselves. This makes it an unpopular choice for some churches, as the success criteria are hard to set and evaluate. I was asked at one training event what the point was if we weren't going to see everyone healed and be able to lay on hands for healing. The point is always in the showing up. The point is that regardless of whether we are broken or not, we are much loved and we are known by name by the One who made us. The saddest thing is to have people in our communities that we only know by label, by what they need, by what is wrong with them. The good news of the gospel is that God accepts us even though we are broken. He calls us by name (Isa. 43:1).

It is that sort of acceptance that we celebrate in our renew spaces.

Some will find healing and recovery in that, some will not. But if it is genuinely OK not to be OK in our spaces, then we have no need of results to see whether regulars are getting better. Our success is just showing up. This takes the pressure off those who are constantly being assessed, and as a result, many report increased wellbeing in the simple act of acceptance and naming.

We therefore call our volunteers 'hosts' and our service users 'regulars'. It is hard to tell on entering a renew space who is who. All are equal and anyone can get you a cuppa, show you around. The hosts are trained to keep an eye everywhere, and ensure simplicity and welcome for all. There is simple training in how to do this well and keep learning to do it better, before starting.

Safeguarding is really important, but as renew spaces do not have a service-user dynamic, this is a simple process of looking at the church's existing safeguarding policy for vulnerable adults and making sure there are good boundaries in each church's policy. An example of this statement is available on our website. Each church has to adapt it, of course, but we have found in our fifty-three centres that in many ways the renew space is the safest and best thought-through space of all the church groups. We are not giving counselling, trying to fix anyone. We are signposting to other services. We don't have any activities that are closed, so anyone can join any group, hence eliminating any coercive or manipulative conversations.

It is such a joy to pop in to renew spaces where a person walking through the door is greeted by name, where they are known, where there is a gentle welcome but where each feels the space is their space.

Being present, truly present, costs us our time, but there is no other way to really attend to wellbeing together. There is no quick fix. These simple, almost monastic, spaces full of hobbies and cups of tea and humans learning how to attend to wellbeing do seem to be having a great effect where churches are willing to slow down, show up and pray.

Questions to consider about being present

1. In what ways are you personally looking after your wellbeing by being truly present?
2. In what ways is your church being present in the community?
3. How can the Five Ways to Wellbeing help you with your own showing up?
4. How could the Five Ways to Wellbeing be used in a shared space in your locality?

7

Be Prayerful

Lord, teach us to pray . . .

(Luke 11:1)

You will be dragged in all sorts of directions by egos and agendas and you will be vulnerable to all that. Your own prayerful habits keep you on your own path.
Rachel Scott, Nottinghamshire County Council

My own prayer habits

This adventure all began with prayer, and prayer is the most important element. It started with my own prayer life, which I had thought was fine. I had been praying all my life; it is like breathing. Interestingly, when I lost my voice it was my breathing that was part of the problem, according to the health professionals and speech therapists at the time. I was a mouth-breather, still am really, and a shallow breather. I learned, with help, to breathe from a deeper place, to avoid shallow breathing, which was circulating germs found in the mouth.

Nose-breathing allows the air entering the body to be filtered through the tiny hairs and thus removes some impurities. Fascinating! Who knew breathing was so complicated!

But that's the whole point, it isn't? Prayer can be like breathing.

Just as with the speech therapists' and occupational therapists' help I learned to breathe properly, more deeply, slower, I was also learning to pray more deeply, slower.

I had been a 'professional pray-er' from a young age, knowing that good out-loud prayers in church got the praise of surrounding adults. I had used prayer to try to fix others. I had done that sort of prayer that is more like 'worrying with your eyes shut'. I had used prayer to preach the sermon no one had asked me to preach. To my shame, I had even used prayer to gossip. I had also had lovely times of intimacy with God, but it was all a bit hit and miss depending on the mood and circumstances that day. Very often, if I am honest, it was the most wor-rying thing that got the most prayer – almost like, if I stopped praying about it, God might forget.

I discovered through long amounts of time in silence that God was content just to spend time with me. Yes, he wanted to hear my prayers and answer them. He wanted to talk with me and direct me. He wanted my confession, supplication and requests.

I'd read lots of books on prayer. A quick Google search on books about 'How to pray' effectively gave me 20 million different options of sites. But to actually learn to pray was a different matter. It was only when other forms of escape had gone – activity, control, talking too much – that I began to learn to really pray!

The habits I was learning involved breath prayer, centring prayer, meditation on a psalm, Lectio Divina, silence and stillness. None of these were comfortable to my charismatic activist mind but all were essential to my weary soul.

After establishing practices that I had learned from retreat centres mentioned earlier, like the Northumbria Community and their excellent Celtic Daily Office and Ffald-y-Brenin and their simple daily rhythms, I settled into a rhythm for myself that involved reading a psalm a week, choosing a phrase that is always good and true to meditate on and sitting with my first cuppa of the day quietly with this phrase. Then I would use Psalm 103:1–5 to settle myself into God's presence before going on to read the Bible or pray about anything else. At noon I would stop and use the Lord's Prayer, pausing after each line to allow the phrase to lead me to pray. Before sleep I would rewind my day with God, using the Examen[1] prayer. This ancient form of prayer was simply rewinding the day with God and spotting signs of his love and beauty and being thankful. Then reading again and letting go of all that was not lovely and beautiful. None of this is rocket science, but just like brushing your teeth or taking a shower, after a while it became second nature even on the days I wasn't 'feeling it'.

A dear friend sadly lost her daughter to cancer a few years ago. She had believed for a miracle – we all had – and was devastated. She hated God and wanted to turn away from her faith. But the day after her daughter died, I remember her telling me she got out of bed and onto her knees and did her morning prayers . . . not because she wanted to, but because it was her habit. Over the months and years of pain and lament that followed, Pat held onto the God who held onto her because she had formed good habits when all was well.

From *my* habits to *our* habits

My habits became shared habits, as the church family I belonged to and some friends and neighbours saw the effect the rhythms were having on me and wanted in. It was also better to have a small community that shared the habits so that there were others to help us stick to them.

This was the basis for the dream for Renew. A place where anyone could join in. I really didn't want exclusive little clubs and inward-facing groups. Praying in this way with others was so good I remember saying it needed to be on prescription. It is interesting now that some GPs are socially prescribing our renew spaces to their patients. Prayer on prescription!

But this way of praying *alongside* not praying *for* means there is no dependency culture established except on

God himself. The habits can be practised anywhere. People can learn to pray for themselves.

Having established that the main thing God was calling us to do was to pray, we gathered our own habits together as a team and came up with a daily rhythm of prayer based on the rhythm we had seen at Ffald-y-Brenin, but simplified, as we knew we were not called to run a retreat centre with staff on hand but a simple accessible space for all in the heart of the town.

There was a certain relief of knowing that if all we managed to do in the space God gave us was to pray then that would be OK. It gave the church some breathing space and took away any sense of panic about over-committing ourselves in a new venture. We were pretty much all hungry for new habits of prayer; most of us knew our own wellbeing would be better served by having somewhere 'chapel-like', somewhere with regular times of quiet and regular times of shared prayer.

For those who knew they wouldn't be able to make it to a physical place, there was at least an enthusiasm around the idea of a dispersed rhythm of prayer . . . joining others in simple prayers when you could, where you were, at set times of the day.

The way in which we got renew37 is a miracle but it was a much smaller space than any of us had imagined. We definitely couldn't hold the sort of meetings that we had been calling 'church' up until that point.

I had seen some amazing social action projects in my quest to lead New Life church in mission. I had also seen beautiful prayer spaces, but rarely had I seen the two together.

The idea behind Renew is that you keep your inner and your outer habits very close and that you make both accessible to all. You don't have little prayer meetings for all the church people to pray for the 'non-Christians' or the poor 'mentally ill people'. You recognize we are all just people and God invites us into his presence together, just as he welcomes us to share our table and hobbies and life.

We had already begun shared habits of prayer in a dispersed fashion. Each member of the church was given a leaflet to stick on the fridge and encouraged to join in with the simple prayers as often as possible.

A simple rhythm of prayer
The rhythm we started with was as follows:

Morning prayer

(8.45 a.m. if possible) for fifteen minutes

Sitting quietly and still in God's presence
Read the psalm for the day
Choose a phrase to meditate on
Use these words from Psalm 103 together:

'Bless the LORD, O my soul, and all that is within me,
    bless his holy name'
(Pause and begin to speak out his name. What do
    you call him? Begin to praise him)
'Bless the LORD, O my soul, and forget not all his
    benefits'
(Pause and thank him for the benefits of knowing
    him today. Short sentence prayers)
He forgives all your sins
(Pause and in the silence confess any known sin and
    receive his forgiveness)
He heals all your diseases
(Offer to him anyone who needs healing, and ask
    for healing for yourself, body, mind and spirit)
He 'redeems your life from the pit'
(Pause and name those people, places and situa-
    tions that feel pit-like – places in the news, etc.)
He 'crowns you with love and compassion'[2]
(Sit quietly and receive his love like a crown for the
    day, his compassion . . . let him fill you so you can
    give love and compassion to everyone you meet
    today)

Often we end here and encourage people to leave quietly so that others can stay and enjoy the love of God in
stillness.

If anyone had any other prayer needs, we would include
them before we finished.

Lunchtime prayer

12 noon

Sit quietly, remind people that the chair is holding them up, just as God is holding them

Encourage people to let any tension go and to become aware of their breathing

The Lord says to you: 'Be still, and know that I am God'[3]

Enjoy a few minutes stillness

Using the Lord's Prayer[4] as a pattern for prayer

The leader (and this is simple so anyone can lead – there is no reading required by all present, in case literacy is an issue) says:

Our Father in heaven, honoured be your name[5]

(Pause and encourage folk to speak out his name)

'Your kingdom come, your will be done, on earth as it is in heaven'

(Pause to consider how amazing that is . . . then speak out the names of places and people on earth needing a touch of heaven)

Give us today our daily bread

(Ask him for what you need, for what others need; praise Jesus, the bread of life,[6] who is enough for us)

Forgive us our sins as we forgive those who sin against us

(Pause and silently confess any sin and choose to forgive anyone who has wronged you. Receive God's forgiveness)

'Lead us not into temptation, but deliver us from
   evil'
(Ask for his leading and pray for the persecuted
   church)
For yours is the kingdom, the power and the glory,
   for ever and ever,
Amen

Gospel reading

To lead into a time of prayer for anything and a time
of blessing for any visitors that day, we sometimes
use the final words of the set prayer for lunchtime
from Ffald-y-Brenin.[7] These rhythms and liturgies
need to be simple, but can be drawn from other
habits and set prayers and most particularly scriptures. Each renew centre may vary in this, but we
strongly commend the Lord's Prayer as a pattern,
as it enables the group to pray more widely than
their own felt needs. We also encourage you to
make sure the set prayer is simple and any extem-
poraneous prayer is kept short and free of jargon
if possible. We are looking to make prayer as accessible as possible to as many people as possible.
As a rule, think about how to make it work for the
person who would struggle the most with lots of
written words to follow.

Evening prayer

> 5 p.m.
>
> Being thankful for the day that has gone
> Start with silence
> Remind folk of the psalm meditation from the
>   morning
> Ask: in what have you seen the love and the beauty
>   of God today?
> Give time for a rewind of the day in quiet and invite
>   people to speak out what they are thankful for or
>   to thank him in silence
> In what have I not seen God's love and beauty?
> Where it is my own fault, I ask forgiveness
> Where it is something I have seen or heard that has
>   disturbed my peace, I give it to God
> A time of open prayer follows
> Choosing one thing God has taught you today,
>   thank him again for the day and speak the words
>   of blessing over each other
> We use the words from Ffald-y-Brenin evening prayer;
>   again you could choose any blessing or evening
>   prayer

These prayer times last about fifteen minutes and all are encouraged to attend who are in the café adjacent at the time. We have found that most people do attend and it is important to make sure you explain carefully what is happening and make it clear that no one is expected to pray out loud.

A prayer time is a natural break in the day and allows you to politely close up and put some boundaries on what you are able to offer. This can be important, as a welcoming space for all can be so open-ended that it becomes exhausting to the hosts.

We started being open Mondays to Thursdays 9 a.m. to 12 noon, beginning and ending each session with prayer. Then we reopened at 3.30 to 5 p.m., again ending with prayer. As time has progressed the space is open pretty much all day Mondays to Thursdays, and it is important at regular reviews to make sure the boundaries are clear so that the project does not become unsustainable.

The wonderful thing about working from a place of prayer is that if anything happens that is difficult or unexpected, there is a lovely, calm prayer space on hand and either individuals struggling can take a bit of time out there or the whole place can stop for a quiet moment if needed. The drivenness is taken out of the work, we work from rest. The café activities are secondary to and spring from the place of quiet prayer.

We do not encourage too much laying on of hands prayer. We prefer people to offer to sit in the quiet alongside and invite God to do his work without too much interference from us. We do offer blessings. This deals with anyone wanting to use the prayer room to manipulate vulnerable people, and also with well-meaning church people putting too much pressure on those who just need to sit quietly with God.

Keep it simple so all can pray

It has been so wonderful to see how many people want to pray, people you might never expect to come and join us. Often the prayer room is full at lunchtime at renew37, and other centres report their mid-session prayer time as being the most popular. Often the still-familiar words of the Lord's Prayer bring peace. People who have never prayed before bring their thanks, their requests, with no churchy words. One lady had learned the Lord's Prayer so she could join us, even though that is not necessary. One person leads with the prayer card, all folk need bring is themselves. But what a delight to hear people who have never prayed before tentatively reaching out to the God who just might be there and just might be listening, and if their friends at Renew Wellbeing are to be believed, just might love them.

There are many stories to tell but they are not mine, so I will leave it to you to visit a renew space one day and hear them for yourself. Telling the stories of others when mental and emotional health is involved feels like a pressure on the subjects of the story to stay in the success part, so we are careful not to tell the stories that are not ours to tell, but to foster spaces where it is safe to tell your own story at any point.

I hope there will be many more stories of people finding God in these simple prayer spaces.

Questions to consider about being prayerful

1. Do you have habits of prayer that you could share? Are they simple enough for anyone to join in? Are they from the Bible?
2. What puts people off prayer meetings?
3. Could you see prayer as part of what you could bring to your community? Where would be a good prayer space?
4. Could you see this linking to a space where other activities happened?

8

Be in Partnership

Working with people of peace

When you enter a house, first say, 'Peace be to this house.' If someone who promotes peace is there, your peace will rest on them; if not, it will return to you. Stay there, eating and drinking whatever they give you . . .

(Luke 10:5–7)

One thing we discovered in our learning was the importance of partnerships, and this is now one of the three key principles of any renew space. Finding and developing a working partnership with existing mental health services is vital. Good partnerships would enable healthy signposting to make sure the offer the church made was simple and sustainable. We set up meetings with mental health professionals who worked in our local council and business owners who were sympathetic to what we were trying to do. We had many coffees, shared all ideas with professionals, listened well for any advice and acted on it where we could.

In seeking to stand alongside friends in the church who were struggling with long-term mental health issues we had become aware that the system was under a lot of strain. I had been to various case reviews and had meetings with local councillors to complain about the lack of support various friends were getting with their mental health issues in the community. The mental health system was oversubscribed, it seemed, and underfunded, struggling to deal with the increasing demand for support in the community. It was clear that complaining and trying our best to support people when the system failed them was not the best we could do.

As a result of one meeting with the council, I was invited to visit the co-production team of our local council mental health service at their centre open to all with lots of great activities going on. It was here that I met those who would take us seriously and help us set up our first renew centre. Finding someone within mental health services is vital for every local church. Our partner in what we did in Nottingham was Rachel. I now know everyone needs a Rachel. She gave up lots of her time to listen to our plans, to advise, to warn, to train and to help us set up good safeguarding procedures. In return we offered her a free place to meet people she was working with and a place to run an afternoon mental health and wellbeing group. She introduced us to the concept of co-production, that is, producing a service together, not 'doing unto' someone.

Rachel explained the concept further: creating a service together, not doing to, but doing with, the lack of power base and how helpful this can be, and we explored how to undo some of the 'them and us' behaviour and language that church groups often have and which can make people feel like projects. Often for all the right reasons, in a desire to show the love of God to others, we unwittingly become the powerful ones and disempower the other.

When discussing the Five Ways to Wellbeing I was able to explain how well the church community does these quite naturally. Faith communities place a high priority on *connecting* with God, each other and their communities. Churches are groups of people on a *learning* journey to become disciples of Jesus. Church groups can organize great *activities* where all are included, walks, outings, meals etc. Prayer and meditation on the Bible are core practices that help us *take notice* of our own feelings and those of the world around us. *Giving* is a central value of a faith community and each is encouraged to find their gifts and offer them in service of each other.

We discussed how often these wonderful community values are lived out behind closed doors, in meetings that are difficult to access or that people think have access requirements that they cannot meet. Rachel also introduced me to a service user who explained how the combination of their psychosis and religious language can also be a very scary experience for people. It had complicated matters for her as a church member, where for all the right reasons, they had done all the wrong things and driven the woman away with their controlling behaviour and language. It was sobering.

This growing partnership with the mental health team through Rachel led to me being invited to their training on positive strength-based approaches to mental health care. I was also invited to be the faith community representative at national discussions in London led by the Social Care Institute for Excellence (SCIE) about preventative mental health care.

Instead of church ploughing a lonely furrow with a reinvented wheel, we began to properly listen to and learn from those who were already working in this vital field. Trust began to grow and by the time we opened the doors at renew37, it was with a clear working partnership with Rachel who runs a mental health and wellbeing group every Monday afternoon at renew37, and makes herself available to our team at regular intervals to review our practice so that we grow as an inclusive community that co-produces for improved wellbeing.

As part of the discussions, we agreed that overtly Christian practices for wellbeing, like prayer and meditation, were really important and that we were not ashamed to say we were Christian. But to make sure the space was accessible to all, we agreed that these practices would be kept to the prayer room so that the café space was for any faith and none. This means that when we pause for prayer, we invite anyone in the café area to join us, but respect anyone's decision not to. We encourage anyone to express their faith as they need to in all areas, but make sure there is as much listening as speaking and that respect for differing views is a key value.

As well as partnering with mental health services, there is value in partnering with local businesses.

Tiffin Tea House next door to renew37 needed kitchen space and we needed prayer space, so the very complicated legal papers were drawn up, and after a long, frustrating process, the two properties were joined with an internal door and work began to make the renew37 side work alongside Tiffin as a café space that would also serve our needs as a church project. This took time and careful negotiations and lots of love. But the outcome has been an excellent partnership that serves both church and local business well. At renew37 we encourage folk to purchase drinks and cakes from Tiffin. We have a kettle and facilities to make simple drinks but want to encourage local business, so we don't sell refreshments.

Tiffin owners have worked hard with us to make the partnership successful, and so far it is working really well. It is a great way for churches to take on space and share rent, and also to avoid having to become a complicated food-producing business themselves.

Finding a good partnership that also blesses the local economy and community like this is not easy to find, but these wonderful people of peace are out there if the church is willing to look and to receive, as well as give.

Engaging with your mental health team: an interview with Rachel[1]

Following is a transcript of a conversation I had with Rachel in 2018, three years after opening our first centre. It sheds light on how a relationship between church and statutory service agency can get started.

> Ruth: I just want to thank you, Rachel, both personally and on behalf of Renew Wellbeing the charity, for all that you have done, going above and beyond your working obligations to support and guide us through the potential minefield of doing something in the area of community mental health. I can say with confidence that we would not be doing what we're doing without your ongoing support and guidance, and so we want to honour you and all that you have given to our movement.
>
> The reason for our conversation today is to explore the journey of the last three years, and draw out advice for other centres across the country who are hoping to find their 'Rachel', because we see developing relationships like this one as fundamental for any group considering setting up a renew centre, and we want to make that as easy as possible.

We know you wear many different hats, but what is your role or title within the council?

Rachel: I work for Nottinghamshire County Council as a community care officer in the community mental health team and have been loaned to the co-production project for two days a week.

Ruth: And how did you hear about renew37?

Rachel: My manager, who leads the co-production team, had a visit from you, Ruth, and because I cover the Rushcliffe area, I followed up the conversation and we arranged our first of many meetings!

Ruth: Yes, lots of structured meetings were the foundation of our working relationship! What in particular drew you to what we were planning?

Rachel: From the outset I recognized the project to be an untapped community resource, with a wealth of skilled individuals and activities for people to join in on. 37 appeared to be a safe support existing outside traditional services. I saw that what you were developing had the potential to be both authentic and holistic. And I also understand individuals' spiritual needs to be a genuine part of their mental health and wellbeing – renew37 seemed to me to be a place filled with really good people who wanted to make a difference; they wanted to help.

Ruth: You are a really open-minded individual and it's been a pleasure to work with you, but how did your department react to you spending time with a faith community?

Rachel: My co-production manager was really positive, but there has definitely been some scepticism… and a few raised eyebrows!

Ruth: So, now people know where to look, what are the essential conversations to have over those first few meetings?

Rachel: We talked about all sorts, it was really important to develop a working relationship and begin to share what motivated and inspired us, but also learn where our boundaries were and set out from the beginning what we were trying to achieve. We discussed:

- *Our views and understanding of the role of mental health services.*
- *Your awareness of who in the church was already using mental health services.*
- *What you understood by spiritual abuse and the damage that has been done by faith communities to people's mental health.*
- *The impact and potential exclusivity of religious language.*
- *The differences in the language we were both using, and where we were or were not willing to compromise around that.*

- *How to tell your story while still respecting another person's story.*
- *What the church community was already doing to support people in need.*
- *Therapeutic risk and how to keep people safe in the space.*
- *Our own understanding of faith and how we view the world differently as a result of our different beliefs and values.*

It is essential to be clear, from the beginning, what the rationale is from a mental health perspective; this may take multiple conversations but everyone must have a clear understanding about what the other is aiming to achieve.

Ruth: You're so right, we did have lots to talk through at the beginning, but that real understanding of each other has formed the foundation of our working relationship. So, thinking of the more practical details now, how much time did you commit to working with renew37, and how was that viewed by the council?

Rachel: Currently I spend four hours a week with 37, I do 1 [p.m.] to 4 [p.m.] on Monday afternoons, and during that time I work with individuals, I facilitate discussions and I also meet Vicki, the centre manager, on a weekly basis to support her development and I meet the church leadership every six weeks to invest in those relationships and ensure we are all on the same page. The council is very positive about the way my work with you is developing and is keen for me to keep investing in the project.

Rachel's top tips for finding the right person to work with:

- Approach the city/county council social care team or local councillor with social care responsibility.
- Look out for the word 'co-production'.
- Check out the SCIE website[2] for blogs and articles about co-production in your local area.
- Find someone willing to take the risk for innovation.
- Look for someone with an occupational therapy background, as they will have group work skills and be able to help you develop a holistic framework to work from.

Ruth: Tell us about the recognition you have received for the work you've done with the centre.

Rachel: I received the Inspire Award for partnership innovation.[3] The council are delighted with the work and the impact of my investment. They have recognized it as a mark of good practice and it's being celebrated on their intranet! I have also recently been asked to join a team to discuss how to implement training across the whole council.

Ruth: What are your top three suggestions for churches wanting to engage with the wellbeing of their communities in this way?

Rachel:

1. *Learn the art of hesitation: if you don't know, don't just jump in! Instead pause and ask for help.*
2. *Don't feel like you have to have all the answers; if you don't know, signpost them to someone who does.*
3. *Don't compromise, stay authentic to who you are and what you believe. Be proud that you are trying to do something different. Don't try to replicate services.*

Ruth: From your perspective, what is the value of each of the Renew Wellbeing core values?

Rachel: Being present is essential . . . it's the unconditional stable base which vulnerable people need to be able to progress, and it's that stability that is so often missing in their lives. Being prayerful provides spiritual choice and it keeps you authentic. You will be dragged in all sorts of directions by egos and agendas and you will be vulnerable to all that. Your own prayerful habits keep you on your own path and will help you weather the storms of criticism.

Being in partnership gives you access to supporting a wider variety of vulnerable people.

Ruth: And finally, what are your own hopes and dreams for the future of partnerships like this one?

Rachel: I'd like to see partnerships grow nationally and see real recognition for the way relationships like this one bring society together. My real dream is for a more compassionate society for all.

Together: Our top tips for partnering with councils and businesses are very simple:

1. Look out for people of peace who are already serving those God has called you to.
2. Start chatting over coffee and do it often before making too many firm plans.
3. Listen and learn. Be prepared to change plans.
4. Hold firm to what you believe are your non-negotiables e.g. prayer room.
5. Be respectful and hospitable while being clear about boundaries and responsibilities e.g. with the mental health team we are not crisis advisors or counsellors and need to be able to signpost people back to the professionals.
6. Keep reviewing, chatting and listening so that problems can be seen as opportunities to learn and change.

Questions to consider about being in partnership

1. Who do you currently consider to be a person of peace in your community?
2. Do you know any people of peace in local businesses?
3. Do you know any people of peace in mental health services?
4. Who could you approach in your community to start a conversation about wellbeing?

PART THREE

Connect

Keep Learning

Get Active

Take Notice

Give

Get Active, Take Notice, Give

Having looked at connecting with the Renew Wellbeing story and the issue of our own wellbeing in the first section, and then addressing the learning around the three principles of Renew Wellbeing, we come to what can actually be done with all this.

What will it look like to slow down, show up and pray? What will it mean to get active, take notice and give?

To *Get Active* as a way to wellbeing will be the only way we see wellbeing renewed in our localities. Keeping our habits to ourselves, not wanting to risk failure, fear of getting too involved may all stop the church from actually acting on the simple invitation to join God in renewing wellbeing.

So this chapter looks at the very simple steps to engage with habits of wellbeing in our communities. This will involve some potential failure, so the next way to wellbeing helps us think about this too.

Take Notice in this context will help build a framework for reviewing and improving what is happening in our renew spaces and also the effect the habits are having on our own wellbeing. This will help keep things simple.

Having outlined the review and improve process, we can use the last way to wellbeing, to *Give*, to help us explore how to join in the spread of the Renew Wellbeing message. This charity has grown and our own wellbeing improves only as we are prepared to share what we are learning – to give. We will look at a growing aspect of the work of the charity in developing hubs and networks so that the church, as one, can learn together.

9

Get Active: Setting Up a Centre

Use this manual to train a team at your church. There are videos on our website to accompany this training. Let us know when you have got started with your pilot project, and we can visit to encourage you and connect you to the Renew Wellbeing family!

The renew centre manual[1]
Quiet shared spaces where it's OK not to be OK
One in four people in our nation have a diagnosed mental illness.[2] Many more are stressed, depressed and anxious. Mental and emotional wellbeing is a key issue for all churches – this is happening in the church as well as in the community. Our local council mental health teams are struggling with the increased demand, and the church has some great things to offer as an inclusive, welcoming community.

If you as a church are wanting to make all that is good about God's family available on the high street to improve the wellbeing of your area, then here are some simple steps to take.

Be present

In the café area, set up one big table to be used for craft and shared learning activities that people might start.

Anyone can suggest or start an activity and over time this is what happens, but to get started you may need to set out a couple of choices and invite people to have a go. For example, we had stone painting and mindful colouring (this is simply colouring-in for adults) out every day for the first few weeks. Now there is more variety, and on some days a led activity is held at the big table.

Have a few other smaller café-style tables, maybe one with sofa seating. Perhaps dot around some card games, books or jigsaws, or if space allows, have clearly displayed activities that people can help themselves to.

The idea is for co-production to be the basis for activities, i.e. working together, not 'them and us', a shared sense of attending to our wellbeing.

Display the Five Ways to Wellbeing in your space. You can find posters to print off and display on the website resources page.[3]

Connect
Keep learning
Get active
Take notice
Give

Use these to make sure you have a balance of activities and in your conversations to see what you need to attend to in your own wellbeing.

It is a good idea to have a chalkboard to display activities and a noticeboard for anything you can signpost people to that would be good for wellbeing.

A display unit or table is essential for all the leaflets and information that signpost people to things that a renew space cannot and should not do. A renew space is a space to show up and be human, a first point of contact, as it were – it is not a service for service users – it is a community space run by the community for the community which is overtly inclusive for anyone with mental and emotional health issues, but will encourage all to take an active part in making the place home.

Having at least two people who are welcoming and friendly and can remember names to act as hosts is essential, and it is best to only open for the hours you know you can commit to, rather than opening all week and then realizing you don't have enough folk from the church willing to show up.

Encourage everyone to come as a human, not a volunteer, and to bring a hobby to share. Discourage churchy talk and exclusive behaviour. By example, show how the space can be welcoming without being loud and 'jolly'. Remember to listen to those with the most lived experience of mental ill health, and get them on team; they are your experts about how safe the place feels.

A host, either paid or volunteer, who is prepared to provide continuity and be the centre manager is essential so that there is good communication across the many folk who will make the place home. The manager will be responsible to find enough hosts and to train them in simple safeguarding.

The link between church and renew space is vital. A renew space cannot exist without a church behind it.

But just a church is not enough to enable good working with people with complex needs.

Be prayerful
Begin to pray.

Listen to what God is showing you.

Develop simple patterns of prayer that anyone could join in with.

Actually use them, even if it's just one or two of you once a week.

Keep to short time periods and be consistent.

Think about where you could pray that is calm and quiet, but where people could find you.

Try praying there.

If you have a premises in mind for a renew space, decide at the start where the larger space will be and begin praying in it at set times before trying anything else. Be silent in the space.

Listen.

When you have a space to pray in that is attached to a space for being present in e.g. a café, make sure the prayer space is simple, big enough for at least ten people, quiet, and accessible easily from the café space.

Ask God to show you how to decorate it with calm, relaxing themes and keep the furnishings simple.

Put up a sign displaying shared prayer times . . . it can be as little as once a week or as much as three times a day. Be consistent.

Make sure there are at least two people committed to show up at those times and that one of them is prepared to take a lead.

Use a simple leaflet or card with the prayer written on it so anyone can lead.

We prefer to have just one card for the leader so people are not concerned with too much print.

Simple is best. More people can join in and no one is excluded.

We use Psalm 103:1–5 every morning.

The Lord's Prayer every lunchtime.

Prayer of Examen every evening.

You are welcome to use our pattern or develop your own.

Encourage silences.

Discourage long prayers or dominating conversations.

Encourage people to enter the prayer room quietly and leave quietly to allow folk who want to stay in God's presence to do so.

Simple instructions at the start, for example:

Welcome to morning prayer. Please feel at home in the silence. Don't feel you have to pray out loud. Relax and know that he holds you. I will lead with a phrase then give time for people to speak short words or sentences after each phrase . . . I will make it clear when that happens. We pray for fifteen minutes and you are welcome to stay here as long as you like quietly at the end, so I would ask you to leave silently when you need to. The kettle will be on in the other room and you are most welcome to stay and chat there, but we keep this space for silent encounters with the God who loves us.

Be in partnership

From the outset, before opening, establish a good working relationship with your local mental health team.

Find out who is in the team. Do you know anyone personally? Talk to those in the church with lived experience to see if you can meet the team with them.

Ask your local councillors to set up a meeting. Or simply ring and ask to meet with someone, particularly someone involved in co-production, or community mental health. Stress that you want to help, to learn, that you are already supporting a number of people with mental health issues, or that you want to help with prevention in your area.

You are looking for a person of peace, not necessarily a Christian. This is someone who is open and warm towards you and who is respectful of your beliefs. This works both ways, of course.

Ask to meet for coffee in a local café, if possible in the place you want to use as a renew space. Explain what you would like to do, being present; having a space that looks like a café but feels like a front room; a place where people can share hobbies and meet each other.

Explain that the church will be paying and that there are volunteers waiting to be inclusive community, but that you know churches have sometimes done harm to vulnerable people and you want help to learn how to make sure this is a safe place.

Don't try to do this in one meeting. You will need at least five meetings before opening your space to make sure there is a strong partnership.

Explain that you would be happy for the team to use the space to run a mental health and wellbeing group in return for help and support as the space gets going. From the outset be clear about the Christian nature of your venture, and that as it is funded by church, you make no apologies for being Christian. Make assurances that no one will be forced to use the prayer room and that any overtly Christian activities will take place in the prayer room so that there is always choice.

We have one afternoon a week when the mental health team make themselves available without referral and run a simple group for folk with diagnosed mental ill health. This has been well used and is making a difference to how often regulars are needing to access medical intervention.

If you were to open less – for example, Renew Ruddington opens one afternoon a week – you could maybe signpost people to a different time when someone would be available, or have someone available at the start or end of each session.

Partnership with local business is also a great way to grow Renew. For some, you will have an existing building that you can make open and inclusive. We suggest a small space, as this is not too overwhelming for anyone feeling anxious. It needs a designated prayer space attached too.

Some of you may want to take on a lease of a high street place or use an existing café premises after hours.

Join the Renew Wellbeing family

Help and advice with all these issues is available from the Renew Wellbeing team. You can visit one of our Renew training hubs (www.renewwellbeing.org.uk/map).

All training is now available online via our website with an online webinar or visit to get the process started, then three training sessions to do together in your church teams before a fifth session with a local area coordinator to get you up and running.

We will keep you updated and connected with weekly emails and meditations, and will gather your stories and reflections to help us learn together as a charity.

If you decide to set up a renew space and your preliminary experiments work out, then Renew Wellbeing would like to invite you to become part of the Renew family. This would involve you agreeing to a set of family values as you set up your renew space to make sure we can offer the concept to local councils with confidence.

Renew Wellbeing, as well as providing ongoing support, advice and materials on the website will also hold regular gatherings and retreats and weekly prayer for national wellbeing.

Visit our website for further information:
www.renewwellbeing.org.uk.

Steps to take

- Visit a renew centre.
- Join a webinar or listen to an introductory talk.
- Pray and establish prayer rhythms.
- Do the training.
- Set up some trial sessions.
- Join the Renew family and have a launch party! Keep in touch and keep it simple!

10

Take Notice: Reviewing and Improving

Be still, and know that I am God.

(Ps. 46:10)

Keep prayer the main thing

All this started with a need to slow down and be present to God. A need to pray and breathe deeply. It is tempting, once a place gets going, to think we have something more or different to offer, and forget to 'be still, and know that [he] is God'. Take notice of your own habits; are you still holding that cup? Are you making use of the prayer space, or are you busying yourself with others to avoid stillness?

As a charity we are seeking to provide, not training days but retreat days, times to listen to God and each other, times to reflect and take notice. We don't have new things to teach, just simple things to remind each other of. We keep in weekly contact with our centres by email, encouraging renew spaces to stick to the psalm

meditations and monthly newsletters to keep connected. There is a Facebook hosts' page to share not just
craft ideas but also in-depth ideas, stories from prayer
rooms, encouragements to remember why we started
this and what the main priority is.

Reviewing your space: how is it going?

We believe this is about depth, not just breadth. To
keep showing up. It helps to regularly review how things
are going, and often a bit of pruning and watering are
needed. A chat with a local coordinator or team member
will help assess what may need pruning back (i.e. stop-
ping when a space gets too busy and complicated) and
what may need watering (i.e. giving a bit more attention).

It can be great to partner with another renew space and
review each other, or to ask a trusted friend to come and
review. The Renew team will try to get to each centre
annually to review and retrain.

Some helpful questions

We ask our renew spaces to send us a completed review
a couple of times a year.

> Being present?
> (which activities are working?)
> Being prayerful?
> (prayer space and prayer times OK?)
> Being in partnership?
> (has the renew space got a contact yet?)

Is it simple?

S: Sustainable

(Are the host team committed to continuing for another six months?)

I: inclusive

(Are all the activities open to all?)

M: Multiplying

(Have any other churches become interested in learning from the renew space?)

P: Prayerful

(Is prayer still the heartbeat?)

L: Love

(Is the quiet, shared space filled with love and compassion?)

E: Equal

(Is it hard to tell who is a host and who is a regular?)

Measuring the wellbeing effect

In terms of success criteria for renewing wellbeing, it is very hard to measure, but we have seen over time in our spaces that there is a rising tide of wellbeing in those centres and churches that have been sticking to these simple habits the longest.

No amount of review processes will help here. The real effect will be on your own wellbeing as you get involved in a renew space and stick at it.

I noticed in my own life that a few months into running the first renew space I was calmer, more able to sit still, breathing more deeply, less anxious about things that didn't matter, more aware of the beauty around me.

The sharing of habits in simple shared spaces will, we believe, have a knock-on effect for the whole church and eventually, we pray, for the whole community.

Although we don't encourage testing and checking all the time to see if wellbeing is improving, we do think it is good practice to ask your regulars, hosts and part- ners to tell you what is good at renew spaces and what needs a bit of work. Decide before you start that if this is co-produced then there is no need to be defensive about criticism. This is a learning zone. All learning is good for us, even if it comes the hard way.

Sharing your own wellbeing

As someone who has got this far with the book and the idea of setting up a renew space, I imagine that you will need to regularly remind yourself, as I have to, what it was that attracted you in the first place. It is so easy to start something well with simple habits and gentle, calm ways and end up driving yourself to succeed, to attract more people, to help more people, to get it right.

The need for wellbeing always starts in our own hearts and lives. We can only share what we know for ourselves. We are always the project . . . no one else.

So in the regular review of the space, I like to ask each host to review their own habits and heart. If things have got a bit stressful it is fine to dial it back and just pray. The rhythms of prayer are essential for peace, and they can be the first thing to slip. It is so easy to see need all around and forget there is a God and it's not us.

Taking notice of how we are using the space, the prayer room and the café area is absolutely key. If we are not enjoying being there it will not feel like a welcoming place to be. Sometimes hosts need to take a break. Always hosts need to make constant use of the prayer space.

11

Give: Multiplying Renew Spaces

Night and day, whether he sleeps or gets up, the seed sprouts and grows, though he does not know how. All by itself the soil produces corn . . .
(Mark 4:27,28, NIV)

We believe this is an organic movement that will spread as each space chooses to give away what they are learning.

Replication

St Giles Church in Northampton have been running a great weekly renew space in their church building for some time now. Denise, their family worker at the time, and Chris, a member of the team, took it on themselves to spread the word to other local Anglican churches and welcome others to come and see what they were doing that was working so well.

Denise designed her own way to train other churches, and within a year they had helped establish four more renew spaces in the Northampton area, taking responsibility to encourage, share resources and visit each other regularly. This delightful development has given us a glimpse of what is possible from each of our renew spaces that are willing to share with others what is working.

If you specifically want to join the Renew Wellbeing movement and become a training hub, here are a few guidelines. Is this you?

Hub churches

A Renew hub church . . .
- is a resourcing church with its own experience of running a renew space for at least a year
- has the capacity to train and support other local centres
- is a centre for training and prayer locally

Each Renew hub church . . .
- has recognized good practice in their own renew centre
- has some capacity to receive visiting teams
- a named coordinator who is coached by the charity director to carry out training
- has the willingness to host prayer gatherings regularly across the year

Renew Wellbeing will . . .

- train and support the hub church coordinator
- provide all materials needed for training
- help cover reasonable travel costs
- provide monthly Skype coaching for coordinator
- provide training and retreats regularly

The Renew Wellbeing core team and area coordinators will prioritize working with hub churches to enable them to replicate well and sustainably.

12

Forging Ahead

When my friend Rob suggested 'Forging Ahead' as the heading for this part of the book, I had my doubts. I have come to dislike any words that suggest pushing, ought to, should do . . . any of those 'pressing in and on' images that made me overwork and undercare for myself in the first place.

Also, 'forging' can mean making a copy of something. In other words, copying something that looks like the first one but isn't. So I am happy to admit that I do want to *forge ahead* in the sense that we want to see the initiative move forward, to see more churches caring enough about those who are anxious, isolated and struggling in their communities to consider doing something smaller and quieter where it's OK not to be OK.

It would seem, however, ridiculous to forge ahead so much in setting up a wellbeing charity that I forget why I set it up in the first place – to stop me forging ahead so much, to slow me down, to present the invitation to other worn-out Christians to slow down, show up and pray.

As I was pondering this final chapter, I was walking up a steep hill. The walk, I had been told, took me to an amazing viewing point of the whole of North Wales – well, maybe not the whole of it, but a good view all the same! I had been walking uphill and down through practically impassable little footpaths for some time, and the idea of forging ahead seemed unnecessary and unpleasant. As usual, my fairly loud internal dialogue was trying to problem-solve and make decisions about why I had got the route so wrong, whether it was worth carrying on etc.

A pause in my prolific overthinking allowed God to place a reminder, a whisper, in my head and heart. I was reminded of an image I had been given, I believe from God, in September 2016 whilst away praying about how to grow from a few centres to helping many churches set up centres at the start of the Renew Wellbeing adventure.

In this daydream – a vision-like experience, really, not something I've had very much of before or since – I was standing in the middle of a vast, empty space. I felt the Spirit of God whisk me up into heavenly places, strip off my old dirty clothes and clothe me in a beautiful gossamer gown over a tight-fitting wet suit, like body armour. Sounds a bit odd, I know, but it gets even more bizarre. Having been clothed and prepared, I was placed back on the empty space which I could now see was a battlefield – and a terrifying one at that. People were falling all around me; the noise and the cries were loud. I felt completely ill-equipped. I had no real armour, no shoes, no weapons. And then I felt the Lord say, 'Dance!'

If you stopped reading at the wet suit bit, it's probably just as well. This was so bizarre but I stuck with it. I was on retreat, I was sitting beside the sea, I had asked God to speak and I had nowhere else to be.

Picnics on a battlefield

So, in this dream I began to dance, whirling around among the brokenness, and I realized I was not alone. There were other dancers, and together we danced, pushing back the darkness and the battle line of barbed wire as we danced. The worship leader beside me, the weapon-carrier (it was my husband in the dream), raised sword and shield to protect us as we danced. And as places cleared on the battlefield, I pointed to each clearing and a group of the dancers set out a picnic mat and sat down. A basket opened in front of them and it filled with good things from the skies. People around began to get up off the ground, put down their weapons, and to join in the picnic.

Clearing after clearing, picnic rug after picnic rug, we danced along the front line until, as I looked behind me, the darkness had become light and the battlefield was becoming a picnic site. It was glorious.

I opened my eyes and felt sure the 'weird vision thing' had not just been too much cheese and sunshine. I don't believe all visions and dreams are significant – mine were usually random results of over indulging and under-sleeping. But this one was different. I instantly knew what it was all about.

I had been praying about renew37 and whether we should and could multiply these renew spaces. I was still leading New Life Baptist Church full-time and trying to work out how to move forward.

It seemed in this dream that prayer and worship were key. Firstly, I was reclothed in robes of righteousness; my own good works just wouldn't do. The significance of the wet suit and gown were from a scripture given to me by my daughter from Proverbs 31:25: 'She is clothed with strength and dignity; she can laugh at the days to come' (NIV).

Not sure which was strength and which was dignity, but I knew this was what I needed to be clothed in to lead a merry dance against the darkness of depression, isolation and despair. God's strength, his dignity do not look like armour but gossamer-thin gowns and the skin we are in. The dancing was most definitely prayer and worship. There was a sense that fixing our gaze, our energies on his presence, his glory, his face was the key thing, the only thing needed.

The darkness of despair, depression and isolation was pushed back as we worshipped. I don't think this was a mandate to sing and dance at people's sadness and despair, rather it was a reminder that the last word is light, not darkness; that there is hope and we can be hope-carriers.

The other dancers, many of them from far and near, I am finding now as I travel around the UK telling folk about

Renew Wellbeing's simple story. Light-bulb moments happen everywhere! God has already called the dancers to dance. So many people are already engaging in the wellbeing conversation, already recognizing the need to slow down and show up, to pray.

The picnic rugs, I think, are renew centres. Safe places in dangerous zones. A place to belong when belonging feels impossible. A place to sit when weariness is over-whelming. A place to see the table spread before you in the presence of your enemies (Ps. 23:5). Just sitting there brought life and healing and repurposing to many. The baskets were filled by God, not us. He provides the peace needed to sustain a renew space. He is the picnic-bringer. But the idea of bring-and-share is implied too. Co-production.

The beauty and simplicity of the whole battlefield begin-ning to change, picnic rug by picnic rug, was what I was reminded of on my slow climb up a big hill the day when pondering this chapter.

I had become content with the sort of growth we had been seeing. From four to forty centres in two years seemed good. But I still couldn't see the promised view. The climb was doing us good but the view was a trans-formed battlefield, light instead of darkness, many picnic rugs. I was reminded that at the time of writing there are more than 50,000[1] churches in the UK so forty renew centres was still in the foothills of the mountain climb. There was a little glimpse of a good view over the trees, but the only way to see the sea and the mountains was to 'forge ahead'.

Higher climb = better view
The climb was long, hard and steep, but the view was breathtaking and completely worth it!

If I had stopped at the first bench and seen the odd tree, I would have missed what I started the walk for in the first place.

This is not a charity wanting to make a name for itself and have a few cafés around the country. This is a charity joining in with the mission of God to renew wellbeing in our nation and beyond through the local church. A wellbeing space on every street would be great. There is more to be done. Forge ahead.

It was obvious as we formed as a charity that to multiply we need to give away what we had learned, and in some ways that's what this book is for. If you are still reading, if you have already taken the challenge to slow down, show up and pray, then you may be wondering how you go from one little centre locally to being able to help others open spaces too. Multiplication happens when after opening one space we are willing to share what we are learning and see other spaces open around us.

To that end, I would encourage some of you to consider not just opening a renew space where you are, but to become training hubs for other churches to learn how to set up and sustain a renew space.

In some areas this is already happening.

Unity: the place of blessing
One of the lovely things that is happening as the movement grows is churches working together. God must love it when his children play nice! I know I do with mine.

The team in Northallerton have worked hard to make sure all five major churches are involved. This meant lots of visits north for me talking with trustees, church leaders, interested church and community members. It meant lots of visits south for them, too, with different groups coming to see renew37 in Nottingham at different times. The result is the Living Rooms project, which I mentioned earlier in this book. A beautiful experiment in Christian unity.

The Churches Together in Towcester also were determined to work together and invited me to come and train them before they had done any of the thinking about where to open etc. God was right there. The next day they were offered a place rent-free on the high street to do a 'pop-up Renew', that is, to set up a renew space for a trial period, and now have funding to carry on there as a churches and community project with extra funding for a manager. It's a great ongoing story of unity in action.

In Ramsey in the Isle of Man, several churches are working together with a local drop-in charity to welcome folk to renew their wellbeing several days a week. It's my home town and a joy to see.

In Purley, as mentioned earlier, the Churches Together group that invited me to speak were keen to work together and have opened a lovely renew space, Renew 23, in the Baptist church building with a joint churches team of hosts. This is with a view to trying it out in one location before multiplying it to various locations. The principle of each church opening one day a week to provide a simple welcoming similar space for those who are anxious or isolated is a really good one and I hope it takes off not just there, but in other towns.

As far as God sees it, there is only *one* church. What a beautiful thing when we find something to unite around. We are all so concerned, so at sea with mental health that it seems an ideal opportunity to share these spaces across a town, to be more consistently present to this need of a place to belong.

Conclusion: A Tsunami of Mental Ill Health, or a Wave of Wellbeing?

This adventure has only just begun.

We believe God is renewing wellbeing and that this current crisis in mental and emotional health provides us with an opportunity as church to rethink how we are being present, how we are praying and how we can partner with local services.

It has been surprising and delightful to have church after church inviting us over the last couple of years to share our story and stand alongside them as they started their own renew spaces. It continues to be very humbling.

It has also been surprising and delightful to have local councils and other charities extend a warm welcome to the efforts of churches, and see their local faith communities as key partners rather than treating them with suspicion.

We do believe having a label that can be trusted on our church-run initiatives will show the partners we are working with that we are prepared to be taught, be in partnership and make sure we look after our boundaries and have safe practice. This will mean services can safely recommend church-run spaces to those they are desperate to be able to socially prescribe. This is an open door for the gospel of wellbeing, of *shalom*, inner peace and of loving community.

We are not trying to establish another Christian charity, we are not trying to build an empire, or a name for ourselves. We are simply the bridesmaid to the heavenly bride – the church.

The church has often been at the heart of each community as a beacon of light, a place of hope and a community of love and acceptance.

It seems that the simple habits of Renew Wellbeing are giving churches all over the nation a simpler, more sustainable way to engage in this key area of need.

It is not a case of the church asking whether they should be involved in the arena of mental and emotional health – we are already involved, because we are human and we are broken.

What if that, and our hunger to practise the one thing, the presence of the God who made, loves, saves and defines us – what if that is all that is needed?

What if it really is as simple as popping the kettle on, bringing a hobby, praying and slowing down together?

We believe it just might be. Let's see a wave of wellbeing reverse this tsunami of mental ill health.

Let's join God in renewing wellbeing in our lifetime and in our own lives and communities.

Your story: an invitation to do less
Just before opening our first wellbeing cafe, renew37, I wrote this prayer in August 2015.

It is one of many written 'psalm-like' poems and prayers I wrote during this time of learning to renew my own wellbeing and offer those renewing habits to others too. More of these simple verses can be found in Appendix 1. Maybe they will prompt you to write some of your own prayers and poems of wellbeing. I have often felt that my story is very ordinary but in telling it I hope everyone will realize that the God of the extraordinary loves to co-produce with ordinary folk like me.

Renew
This, the first of my poems, is still my prayer and I invite you to pray it with me and to join in becoming the answer:

> I can see a place
> Where all are welcome
> Where family is beyond blood
> Where those who thought they had the least to say
> Least notice taken
> Became most loved

Most honoured
A place where all seek God
All seek and find
His beautiful presence
And become viral carriers
Infected with his sweet love and grace
A place where we all acknowledge ourselves as broken
No labels are necessary
Other than human and loved
Where sin is acknowledged
And left behind
And sadness is allowed to be what it is
For as long as it needs to be
Where honesty is the native tongue
And being transcends doing
Where sitting quietly with yourself and God is valued
As much as busying yourself with others
Where the other is seen
Through the eyes of the God
Who made them
And are loved with his compassion
Where simplicity
Gentleness
And joy live
And God is not privatized into meetings
Where we become, all of us
Young and old, co-creators with him
Of small things of beauty
And large systems of justice

Of little works of art
And big works of courage
A place to dream
To imagine
To dare
A place to rest
And pause
And be
A lump of yeast of kingdom life
Carrying the DNA of Christ
To every home and workplace
A quiet shared place
Where it's OK not to be OK
And where being present, prayerful and in partnership
Breed hope, love and peace.
Where one place
Becomes many places
A web of wellbeing across the nation
I can see a place

Appendix 1: Poems and Psalms

Here are a few of my own poems and thoughts. Some might call them psalms.

In attending to your own wellbeing, you may find it helpful to use a journal to write your prayers. I have certainly found the poetic form to lend itself well to things that are hard to express in prose. Some of my concepts explained in the chapters of this book around wellbeing may make more sense to the poetic among you in these verses. Do have a go at your own. They don't have to be perfect, just honest.

The Seesaw
This is my response to finding out that many mental health professionals believe that just balancing resources and challenges will lead to wellbeing as the small balance point in the centre of the seesaw lines up. What is your response to the various definitions of wellbeing?

What if the seesaw never steadies?
What if the challenge weighs you down?
What if resources seem too distant?
Struggling to hide that inner frown
What if there is no trick to balance

Habits and happenings fight in vain
What if the moment that you find it
Balance escapes, unhinged again
Surely if our God is stronger
No battle is too great
The see should never saw
Why do I feel so overwhelmed
When his great weight should overwhelm it all
Try harder to gather God's resources
and pile them on the wobbly victory end
Let go
Let God
Come on, child, grow
Get off the ground
He is not found so low
No!
Wellbeing is not tight and mean
Its vast expanse embraces all
Arms wide upon a cross
Tomb empty
So from the seesaw fall
And know he is not just a tiny balance point
He is the very ground beneath your feet
He catches you
You catch your breath
It's his air you breathe
He is above
Below . . .
He's all
In all
'In him we live and move and have our being'[1]
Wellbeing

Dwellbeing
He dwells in us and in him we hide
Then the dwelling
Takes the seeing and the sawing
In its stride

Dwellbeing

This is a word I coined to try to express something of the depth conveyed by the word 'wellbeing'. In this poem I examine the connections necessary for wellbeing with God, the world around us, others and ourselves.

How lovely is your dwelling place[2]
His dwelling place
'Your glory fills the whole earth'[3]
Yes, the whole earth
You dwell in ocean depth
and mountain height
in fragrant flowers
and eagle flight
in tiny bugs
and vast blue skies
How lovely
His dwelling place?

We 'are being built together into a dwelling place for God'[4]
The church
His choice of dwelling place
Cement between the cracks
In varied personalities
Choosing to share

To work, to care
To love
In all its crazy forms
Regardless of our preference
And complaint
He dwells in us *together*
And we are made for this
Edifice of brokenness
Not all harmonious bliss
In meetings and in silence
From mud stuck to free
In contention and compassion
How lovely
His dwelling place

He 'dwells in you' by his Spirit[5]
You, the other
Yes, I see his glory
His presence
Reflected in your eyes
You – his love, his joy, his prize
His beauty in the smallest hint of hope
The bravest acts of courage
In sharing how you cope
In shared spaces where
Each I meet shows signs
Of the Master's hand
Masterpiece-making
How lovely
His dwelling place

'It is no longer I who live, but Christ lives in me'[6]
Me
His dwelling place
Lovely?
Now, that's a stretch
For mind and heart
Where shall I start
To realize that I am lovely too
In my skin
The skin he is in
I choose to live this day
And tend the beauty
As I would his earth, his church, the other
To be as careful with myself
My body, mind and spirit
As I hoped to be with nature's best,
My family and the church
My life
His dwelling place
My thoughts
My feelings
My cheers and cries
My choices
His life in me
His dwelling place
How lovely
Statement not question
His words
His time
His dwelling place
The earth, the church, your life and mine
How lovely!

Now Someone Knows My Name

Written in response to one of our regulars at renew37 telling us that she could go all week without hearing her name mentioned. The first line is inspired by Isaiah 49:16.

My name inscribed on eternal palms
My days
Written and planned, held in stronger arms
Our name
His church
Sweet bride, chosen one
His name
Our battle cry
And soul song
This name
Above all other names
In whom our name belongs
For unnamed, unknown, unloved ones
Who spend a day
A week, a year
Not hearing
They are loved
And often when their name is heard
The name that came
With life breath at created word
That precious name
Called out
In clinical spaces attached to notes
From officious faces
For those whose labels show before their names
Who have not heard

The whisper of the Father, Spirit,
Son who came
The ones who no one knows their name
He calls you, 'Bride, come out
From death-filled tomb' and breathing in his life
Breathe out
And make some room
A room
A space
Where all are known
By name and face
And where his name is never far but near to all
And where we hear his call
Come out
Come near
Come back
Come here
My child
My bride
Beloved and blessed and named
My name
Your name
Our name
All held within the name above all names
And in this name 'we live
and move
and have our being'[7]
Wellbeing
Dwellbeing
To dwell in him and him in me
And there to find each other free

His offspring
Bound in love and grace
Where each is known and loved
and finds their place

Be Present

Be present
Presence
Just showing up
Surely there's more to it than that
Just being there
Staying in a moment
With another
Without agenda
Presence
Better than our gifts and presents
What better can we give another being
Than our being
With them fully
In their story
One human being to the other
Presence
Surely this is what we believe
What we seek
What we long for
What we practise
The 'Word became flesh'[8] and he is present
Presence
As we embrace this moment
Not the next
We choose to be present
To the one who is ever-present

And in doing so we become his presence
To the ones for whom
Presence is the greatest present of all

Be Prayerful

To pray
Is to breathe
And in breathing know
The warmth of your breath.
On us
In the stillness
To pray is to say
Anything and nothing and
To know as we are known
Spending time where love, not words, are the currency
To pray
Is to ask
Believing he is good and he longs to give
To pull up a chair to the table with Jesus
And another for the stranger
And to cry out for the thing that breaks our heart
And to wait, knowing
He hears
He cares
He answers

I wrote the poem below as a response to the beautiful question the disciples ask Jesus in Luke 11, not 'How can we multiply bread?' or 'How can we raise the dead?' – they had spotted the secret, his time alone in prayer, and asked, 'Lord, teach us to pray . . .'

Lord, Teach Us to Pray

*Now Jesus was praying in a certain place, and
when he finished, one of his disciples said to him,
'Lord, teach us to pray . . .'*

(Luke 11:1)

Lord, teach us to pray where prayer is breath
We pause
And in the pausing
Know that you were always there
Breathe deep
My soul
The air of his presence
Will not run out
This breathing underwater
Not from tank or tube
But with new lungs designed by him to inhale love
Don't gasp and grasp
This drowning is not death but life
The job you made of breathing by yourself,
Of quickly gulping pockets of fresh air
Is done
Be still
Be still, my soul, and know that he is God
And you are not
He does not need your conjuring or your pleading
To be there
He is the air
In which you live
To know him
Really know him

And to make connection with the source
That came
And moved into our space, our time
Now that is breathing, that is life
Connect and learn
And in your learning
Grow and act and move and be
And taking notice of the things you see
Of those around you who can't breathe
Give life and breath
as freely as received
Breathe deep my soul breathe daily, hourly, often
pause
and so together say
Lord teach us to pray

Be in Partnership

People of peace
Thank you
That you seem to have heard
Something we missed
Although we deem you not to know the voice
It seems that you are there
Where he is at work
While we are in meetings asking where he is
People of peace
We join you
In a broken world
Where you have already rolled up your sleeves
And learned a thing or two
While we wait for a reinvented wheel
Behind closed doors

People of peace
Teach us what you know
And we will join you
To serve the lost and the broken
And maybe
Just maybe
You'll meet Jesus in the joining

Rachel

A few words about the first ever partner in mental health services to take us seriously and realize the potential of partnering with the local church community.

Thank you, Rachel.

Have you got a Rachel?
She's not in the church
Because she didn't think she'd find the answer there
She rolled up her sleeves and
answered the cry we were missing
And now she knows a thing or two we don't
So let's not assume
Let's listen
And ask
And be humble
And learn
Because the church needs Rachels
And those Rachels need the church.

Appendix 2: Good Practice

Safeguarding

Safeguarding is about appropriate boundaries: physical, emotional and spiritual. It includes safeguarding the reputation of the centre. Safeguarding is not a bureaucratic necessity but is life-giving and vital to the flourishing of the centres, all those who attend: hosts, guests, regulars and partners.

1. **The host team and regulars.** For all to feel safe, the centre values must be upheld and all be treated with respect. Safeguarding is essential to maintain a safe space. Each church setting up a centre will have a Vulnerable Adults safeguarding policy, and will need to train all hosts using this policy and their own training procedures. Added to this will be a Renew paragraph specific to the centre written by the church and Renew team in partnership with a mental health professional. It is important for the church running the renew centre to follow up this training with their own safeguarding training for *all* hosts.

2. **Safeguarding and team relationships.** It is vital that all team members can express any concerns they have. Each centre should have an external advisor or chaplain (this can be a church leader/member, or

someone from another local church). They will meet with the team on a regular basis and will be available to any individual who has a concern.

3. **Safeguarding and keeping yourself safe.** It is vital to make sure you keep yourself safe at all times. If you don't feel comfortable, you need to ask yourself why, and take action. It is important to prioritize your own wellbeing to be an effective host. Use the prayer space, join in the activities, do not over-give. You also are human!

Each renew space is covered by the safeguarding policy of the church that supports it, and the hosts will need to be DBS checked, i.e. to have a police background check, and trained in accordance with that policy.

Appendix 3: Stories from Wellbeing Centres

Here are some stories of a few renew centres and the journey that God has taken other churches on to be present, prayerful and in partnership in their communities.

It is tricky to tell other people's stories. We are dealing with sensitive issues and trust is key. All the folk mentioned below have given their permission to have their stories included. There are so many more stories of big struggles and even bigger grace. Because we believe it is OK not to be OK, we don't want to just tell stories of those who begin to improve in their mental health. They are not valued more than those who remain unwell but are courageous enough to keep getting up each day. I am so grateful to the hosts who have taken time to give me these reflections. They are written in their own voices, not mine.

Renew 127, Bentley, Doncaster

Anne G's story:

Somewhere during 2015 a thought popped into my head about retiring from a job I absolutely loved and had been doing since 1997, a job which God in effect got for me – but that's another story.

So, with my sensible head on, I dismissed the idea, especially given that the government moved the goalposts and I wouldn't get my state pension until I was 66. I was 59 at the time. So, I studiously ignored the voice that was telling me to retire, but consequently I signed myself up for retirement course in November 2015.

I made plans to retire and then come back for three days a week, as had happened for others, but that door closed. The retirement thought persisted until in the end I gave in and signed all the paperwork and left the NHS on my 60th birthday in May 2016. Now, bearing in mind that I was first to arrive and the last to leave work, that I had built up a telephone caseload (I was a secretary, not a practitioner), that I loved communicating with our patients, that when I knew patients were in for appointments I would personally greet them and find out how they were, but most importantly that I was totally fulfilled and this was where God had put me, why did I find it so easy and so right to leave?

I left work and slipped seamlessly into retirement. Even *I* had trouble understanding how easy the whole process of leaving had been.

Fast forward to September 2016 when Ruth Rice came to our church (Bentley Baptist Church in Bentley, Doncaster) to talk about Renew. As she spoke my heart burned within me and the scales dropped from my eyes. I had been nineteen years in training 'for such a time as this' (Esth. 4:14) and this was the reason that it had been so easy to retire.

During the presentation, mental health was discussed and there was much talk about what we could expect. There was a lot of fear and trepidation. At this point I was propelled forward to talk about the nineteen years I'd spent working as a secretary to a consultant psychiatrist. My experience, personal and at work, had led me to a greater understanding and empathy with those who suffer with mental health problems, who are isolated as a consequence of their illness, who are stigmatized because of their illness, who are judged because of their illness and told to get a grip or 'pull yourself together' – as a person who suffers from depression and takes antidepressants to keep it at bay and to enable me to function daily, do people really think that if I could pull myself together I would choose not to?

I also reassured our church that people who suffer with mental health problems are ordinary people, and yes, there are extreme cases, the ones we read about in newspapers, but these are a minority and not a barrier to setting up a renew centre.

So, our church decided that we would pursue the matter further and look for premises. In early 2017 we looked round an old bookmakers' shop. It was a dump and I for one could not see the potential; it was dirty and in poor repair, there was a safe concreted into the space we wanted for a quiet room, and there was a pillar in the middle of the room that couldn't be removed. Nevertheless, we proceeded and finally after long negotiations and dealings with the Baptist Union, Yorkshire Baptist Association and the solicitors for the bookmakers, we finally got the key to the premises in July 2017, right in the middle of the holiday season! Renovations began in September 2017 and after a lot of hard work, we finally opened our doors on Tuesday 23 January 2018.

I can honestly say that from the time we opened, there has never been a day when we haven't had someone through our doors. We have met and made friends with many lovely people; we have laughed together, cried together, prayed together and signposted people to relevant services, who in turn have provided what is needed.

We are in partnership with various agencies who meet with us regularly; we have carers who bring their clients; the residents of the local sheltered housing unit come and see us for coffee and a chat, with or without a worker.

To date we have had a grand opening by the Mayor of Doncaster, hosted a MacMillan Coffee Morning, held an afternoon tea for our lovely new friends, decorated our space for Armistice Sunday, made numerous Christmas decorations and painted lots of pebbles – we also decorated our space for the Tour de Yorkshire which passed by our premises in May 2019, and was a great success with our community.

In reality we are a group of individuals with a desire to love all those in our community who feel excluded, who are lonely, who are misunderstood, who suffer with mental health problems in silence. Our centre, Renew 127, provides a quiet, safe space where it's OK not to be OK, and to be accepted for who you are: no judging, just acceptance.

One lady who was an ex-drug addict said that what she loved about our places was that no one judges. Another chap came back months later and said to our Tuesday staff that this place had saved his life, helped him to understand that it was indeed OK not to be OK, and had given him the courage to take steps to change his life. Our Tuesday staff said that the transformation in him in all areas was amazing. One of our visitors, told me that from the first visit she found the staff to be friendly and very welcoming. She further added that she had made new friends in the centre and felt comfortable in our space. She also loved the fact that we welcome children. One of her children said that they had a colouring book, met new people, played Connect Four with the staff and learned to play draughts too. This lady also loves coming in for rhythm of prayer and amazingly contributes really well.

Renew 55, Chipping Campden, Gloucestershire

Tooty's story:

Our Renew journey began when I heard Ruth give a presentation at the Fresh Streams[1] conference at The Hayes Conference Centre in Swanwick (a missional Word and Spirit network for leaders who have been foundational for Renew Wellbeing in giving courage and support), but at the time couldn't imagine how the great things happening at renew37 could translate into working for us here at Campden.

The seed was sown, but lay dormant for quite a while.

I was (and still am) involved in running a foodbank at the church, and knew that every person who came in was, at the very least, depressed, but more often than not they were at their wits' end and suffering from various mental health issues. I believed that we as a church could and should be offering more to people in such dire states so my friend and I started weekly prayer walks in Campden, always asking God to show us what he wanted us to do, and praying that we would be obedient if it was something we felt was beyond us!

Can't remember the exact moment, but I'd heard Ruth speak a couple more times, and then, Christmas 2017, we came across Renew Wellbeing, we believe God led us to it, and we've been focused ever since.

We opened Renew 55 in October 2018 and from week one, we had referrals from the local mental health team, who had not even met us! Our guests come not only from Campden, but also from Broadway, Mickleton, Blockley and Badsey.

If I'm honest, I can't pretend the enemy hasn't been at work, trying to undermine us at times, but God has been and is being so faithful to us at Renew. We pray for courage and strength to keep moving and growing . . .

Renew Nailsea, Somerset

Margaret's story:

On the surface, Nailsea appears to be a town full of comfortable, middle-class families, devoid of the need experienced in many more urban contexts. Dig a little deeper, though, and you discover a higher than average number of single-occupancy households, highlighting a problem with loneliness. Dig a little deeper still, and you discover individuals and families struggling to sustain an image in keeping with the town, desperately trying to make ends meet while smiling on the outside. Then there are those who are drowning in the attempt to hold it together, marginalized and forgotten by most of the local community.

Opening a renew space enabled us to welcome those who are desperately seeking companionship, a place to laugh, to enjoy a warm drink, to be welcomed by name and invited to join in. Having opened in February 2019, we have a small but growing community of different ages and life experiences. It has been great to experience how this community support one another and follow up on one another's ups and downs each week. Games are particularly popular in our space at the moment, and it's been great to witness how games such as dominos and 'Uno' can bring together folk from such contrasting situations, from lonely older friends, those battling with addictions, and those who just appreciate a place to go where they are known by name.

Prayer is a grounding time, particularly the lunchtime prayer. Some join us specifically for this, others stay on to listen, and a few stay on the margins but seem to enjoy the peace of that time. Ensuring a welcome for all is not without its challenges – some people's needs and ways of being can conflict with another person's – but maintaining an open door, with a welcome smile and a particular emphasis on calling people by name is working. As a host, there is a lot of watching and listening required, but being present and taking a real interest in each person, able to move between conversations as necessary, helps us to really journey with people through life's challenges and to ensure the space stays safe and welcoming for all.

Welcome looks different for different people. For one, it is a listening ear, allowing them time and space to offload, and sometimes to pray. For another, it is about knowing what they like to drink and making it just how they like it. For still another, it's being served a drink when most of what they experience in the week is unkindness and rejection. It's about being invited to the table and given the opportunity, and the choice, to join in. It's about playing a game with others, sometimes for the first time in many years, and laughing together. It's about creating something that looks half-decent and may bring joy to someone. Sometimes it's about losing, or messing up at craft, or spilling a drink, and still being able to smile and laugh and be accepted.

We still have work to do. We need to keep building our team so that the load is shared more evenly, keeping the edges blurred so that there is space for all to participate in building community. We need to engage the church community more actively in prayer and support and awareness of those who visit our space, enabling them to develop a greater understanding of wellbeing, not only in relation to our renew space, but ensuring that as a church we have a healthy understanding of wellbeing that permeates all that we do.

Wellbeing Café, Broughton Astley, Leicestershire

Jonathan's story:

I had heard stories of Renew before, and heard of someone setting one up which was great but didn't resonate with me. A year or so later, Ruth was speaking at an East Midlands Baptist Association Day and it began to put some form and content to things I had been thinking and praying about, a café of sorts, in our future church redevelopment. Our present building wasn't really viable. Speaking with Ruth, she suggested doing something in the community. I ended up casually chatting with the local councillor, who was thrilled with all I was sharing and said they could give us a space! The council voted in favour and has provided a room in the village hall free of charge for six months. Their comment was that promoting wellbeing is one of their mandates/values, but they don't have the resources. However, by partnering with our church in providing a space, they are able to do that.

Renew 169, Towcester, Northamptonshire

Laura's story:

It was early in 2018 that my minister excitedly gave me details of a wellbeing café network called Renew Wellbeing, and told me to ring Ruth Rice, the organizer. I went to visit her in Nottingham at the first café that she had set up. So struck was I by the simplicity of the model and the clear needs it was meeting that I took the idea to Churches Together in Towcester. We decided that this was what the town now needed – a quiet, shared space for anyone struggling with emotional or mental health, where 'it's OK to not be OK'. Don't we all have days like that?

Ruth came to visit us shortly after this in Towcester to do some training. I'd noticed a venue on the high street that had been vacant for a long time, and as I walked back to the car park with Ruth that night, we went past it. I joked that it was where I thought the café should be and she took a photo of me outside and I laughed, never thinking it would happen. There are stories about people laughing at God's suggestions in the Bible;[2] be careful what you laugh about!

Fast forward . . . we received the keys to the property on 19 October 2018 and the landlord agreed to provide the property to us rent-free for six months. There was an amazing community response to pleas for painters, furniture, plumbing, DIY jobs and so much more, which enabled the vacant shop to be transformed from a damp, drab mess to a place of light, homeliness and welcome. We opened our doors to guests on 12 November for two afternoons a week and have had a steady stream of people ever since. We had 197 people visit in the first three months of opening.

We have now accessed grants worth £80k to enable us to pay rent for three years and to employ a café manager to expand the variety of wellbeing-related activities that happen in the café. It's an exciting adventure that God is taking us on and he is with us every step of the journey. And I saved the best until last. What I never envisaged was the huge impact that volunteering in the café has . . . on those involved! It's been such an amazing blessing to be part of this project, and going into the café each week with anticipation about who you might meet is not only exciting, but it's relaxing and forces us to take time out of our busy lives to just *be*. Journeying alongside others at difficult times of their lives is a privilege. And for me, I've been on a journey through therapy to address childhood trauma and symptoms of PTSD over these last two and a half years, and I've no doubt that God put the idea of the wellbeing café into my life at the most perfect time. Being involved in setting up the café enabled me to feel established and connected in my town, and it's been in giving to the café and through meeting the remarkable people that make use of that café space that I have received the most healing on my journey.

See our website for a list of current renew centres: www.renewwellbeing.org.uk

Appendix 4: Great Courses and Resources

As well as opening a space, your church will need to think and pray around their attitudes to mental health. We recommend these courses for use in church groups, not renew spaces.

The Wellbeing Course by Dr Michele Hampson
Wellbeing with a Christian Perspective Participant's workbook and leaders manual, available on the resources page of our website: www.renewwellbeing.org.uk

This is a wonderful resource for churches; a simple look at wellbeing written by a great friend of Renew Wellbeing with many years' experience in psychiatric medical practice as well as now being a curate in the Anglican church. A rare and wonderful person with understanding of both worlds . . . the church and the mental health system. Michele works with Renew Wellbeing as our advisor.

The Sanctuary Course
By Sanctuary Ministries, Vancouver:
sanctuarymentalhealth.org

A new resource for all churches to help them sustain their own wellbeing and their presence, prayerfulness and partnerships – *free* and great for any small-group setting.

The Sanctuary Course is an eight-week online resource with great videos and great questions covering topics such as self-care, community, wellbeing, and stigma.

Renew Wellbeing loves to partner with Sanctuary Ministries and thoroughly recommend this course to all our churches.

TalkThrough
TalkThrough offers a combination of resources that aim to equip youth workers, parents, churches and schools to attend to wellbeing issues. Renew Wellbeing is working with TalkThrough to develop training for renew spaces for children, youth and families. Renew Children, Youth and Families (Renew CYF).

To know more about the work at TalkThrough, please check out their website: www.talkthrough.org.uk

Kintsugi Hope
Kintsugi Hope, a charity set up by Patrick and Diane Regan in 2017, exists to make a positive difference to people's emotional and mental wellbeing. Kintsugi Hope regularly holds or takes part in speaking events, raising awareness on mental health and stigma as well as acting as a driving force to open up conversations on topics

many find difficult. Kintsugi Hope also trains people to run Kintsugi Hope Wellbeing Groups in their community in its commitment to reach out to the broken and lonely.

To find out more about their work and events: www. kintsugihope.com

Livability

Livability offer training and resources to support churches in becoming places where everybody can take part. As a Christian disability charity connecting people with their community, Livability want to build wellbeing for the whole congregation, promoting the participation of all. They provide support to churches and organizations who are exploring mental health and wellbeing, offering a range of tailored workshops. To contact Livability, email joinin@livability.org

Mind and Soul Foundation

A great charity that seeks:

To educate: sharing the best of Christian theology and scientific advances.

To Equip: Helping people meet with God and recover from emotional distress.

To Encourage: Engaging with the local church and mental health services. www.mindandsoulfoundation.org

Image by Mark from Renew 5 at the Living Rooms in Northallerton who sadly died in February 2020.

The Living Rooms family are so proud of Mark and the gifts he gave us through his photography in particular. He has left a beautiful legacy which we will all treasure.

About the Author

Ruth Rice is Director of Renew Wellbeing, a Christian charity started in 2017 with help from Cinnamon Network. She lives in Nottingham with husband Mark and they have three grown-up children and a small neurotic dog. Born in the Isle of Man, Ruth has been a Christian since she was a little girl and was a primary school teacher for twenty years, then led New Life Baptist Church full time before starting the charity.

Ruth set up the first Renew café in Nottingham in 2015 in response to her own and others' needs for a 'quiet shared space where it's OK not to be OK'. Following a long bout of burn-out Ruth found calm habits of prayer, meditation and creative hobbies really helped, and she longed to share this new peace with her church and community.

Renew37 in West Bridgford, Nottingham, was set up four days a week by New Life Baptist Church and is still going strong. Giving up the day job to set up the charity enabled Ruth to help other churches explore Renew cafés and before lockdown there were fifty-three cafés operating nationally. Ruth is believing for many more coming out of lockdown. The charity provides free training through its website www.renewwellbeing.org.uk.

The simple welcome, 'bring a hobby, share a hobby' and the prayer space kept open at all times with a rhythm of prayer on offer throughout the day has seen many people finding peace. Renew Wellbeing works on three principles: be present, be prayerful and be in partnership with mental health services.

Ruth longs for every church to find ways to bring God's peace onto the high street and open spaces for all to attend to their wellbeing. One regular at renew37 summed up the beauty of such a simple approach like this: 'We walk alone without someone to care . . . but now I have found friends, a new family in a new place! Thank you all! Such a blessing – a safe place in a crazy world . . . wonderful people. *Someone knows my name!*'

With thanks to New Economics Foundation and the Government's Foresight project who funded the Wellbeing work. http://neweconomics.org/2008/10/five-ways-to-wellbeing-the-evidence/.

Bibliography

Bonhoeffer, Dietrich, *Life Together* (London: SCM Press, 1954).

Boyd, Greg, *Present Perfect* (Grand Rapids, MI: Zondervan, 2010).

Brown Taylor, Barbara, *Learning to Walk in the Dark* (Norwich: Canterbury Press, 2015).

Brueggemann, Walter, *The Prophetic Imagination* (Minneapolis, MN: Augsburg Fortress, 2001).

Coleman, Kate, *7 Deadly Sins of Women in Leadership* (Birmingham: Next Leadership Publishing, 2010).

Cordeiro, Wayne, *Leading on Empty* (Minneapolis, MN: Bethany House, 2009).

Godwin, Roy, and Dave Roberts, *The Grace Outpouring* (Eastbourne: David C. Cook, 2012).

Greig, Pete, *How to Pray* (London: Hodder and Stoughton, 2019).

Johnstone, Matthew and Ainsley, *Living With a Black Dog* (London: Robinson, an imprint of Little, Brown Book Co., 2008).

Kelly, Gerard, *Spoken Worship* (Grand Rapids, MI: Zondervan, 2007).

Nouwen, Henri, *Reaching Out* (Grand Rapids, MI: Zondervan, 1998).

Nouwen, Henri, *The Selfless Way of Christ* (London: Darton, Longman & Todd, 2007).

Regan, Patrick, with Liza Hoeksma, *Honesty Over Silence* (Farnham: CWR, 2018).

Rupp, Joyce, *The Cup of Our Life* (Notre Dame, IN: Ave Maria Press, 1997).

Scazzero, Peter, *Emotionally Healthy Spirituality* (Nashville, TN: Thomas Nelson, 2006).

Seligman, Martin, *Authentic Happiness* (London: Nicholas Brealey Publishing, 2003).

Swinton, John, *Spirituality and Mental Health Care* (London: Jessica Kingsley Publishers, 2001).

The Northumbria Community, *Celtic Daily Prayer: Book Two* (London: Collins, 2015).

van der Hart, Will, and Rob Waller, *The Power of Belonging* (Eastbourne: David C. Cook, 2019).

Wax, Ruby, *A Mindfulness Guide for the Frazzled* (London: Penguin Life, 2016).

Wenham, Gordon, *The Psalter Reclaimed* (Wheaton, IL: Crossway, 2013).

Willard, Dallas, *Renovation of the Heart* (Nottingham, UK: IVP, 2002).

https://neweconomics.org/2008/10/five-ways-to-wellbeing-the-evidence (accessed 29 May 2020).

Notes

Introduction
[1] A regular at renew37 wellbeing café.
[2] www.england.NHS.uk (accessed 26 May 2020).
[3] Origin of phrase not confirmed but thought to be first used commercially in 2011 by Hope for the Day, www.hftd.org (accessed 29 May 2020).
[4] www.neweconomics.org and https://www.gov.uk/government/publications/five-ways-to-mental-wellbeing (accessed 12 December 2019). Permission given to use 5 Ways to Wellbeing with thanks to New Economics Foundation and the government's Foresight project.
[5] Esther 4:14.

The Renew Story
[1] A regular at renew37.

1 My Story
[1] God's whisper during a dark time.
[2] https://www.new-wine.org/ (accessed 26 May 2020) is a national conference where healing is often offered, and that particular year my voice loss was completely healed overnight after months of struggling with no voice.

[3] Joyce Rupp, *The Cup of Our Life* (Notre Dame, IN: Ave Maria Press, 1997).

[4] Dietrich Bonhoeffer, *Life Together* (London: SCM Press, 1954).

[5] NIV UK 2011.

2 The renew37 Story

[1] Matthew 18:20, KJV.

3 The Renew Wellbeing Story

[1] A regular at renew37.

[2] www.cinnamonnetwork.co.uk (accessed 21 May 2020).

[3] *Dragon's Den* is a TV programme in the UK where people are invited to present innovative ideas to potential investors to try and secure their backing.

[4] Kate Coleman, *7 Deadly Sins of Women in Leadership* (Birmingham: Next Leadership Publishing, 2010); www.nextleadership.org (accessed 26 May 2020).

[5] www.freshstreams.net (accessed 26 May 2020). A missional network of church leaders who gather at different times across the year particularly in January at The Hayes Conference Centre in Swanwick. Fresh Streams has always been 'home' to me; a group of like-minded friends on a journey who always give me courage and help me follow God's leading.

[6] See Matthew 14:13–21.

5 What is Wellbeing?

[1] https://www.mind.org.uk/information-support/your-stories/what-is-mental-health-and-mental-wellbeing/ (accessed 29 May 2020). Used with permission. © Mind. This information is published in full at mind.org.uk.

[2] www.whatworkswellbeing.org/about-wellbeing (accessed 30 May 2020). Used with permission.

3 Martin Seligman, *Authentic Happiness* (London: Nicholas Brealey Publishing, 2003).
4 See Michele Hampson's teaching on this. Resources page, www.renewwellbeing.org.uk (accessed 25 May 2020).
5 See Rupp, *The Cup of Our Life.* Used with permission.
6 Brother Lawrence, *The Practice of the Presence of God* (Eastford, CT: Martino Fine Books, 2016).

6 Be Present

1 New Economics Foundation and the Government's Foresight project who funded the work. More details at http://neweconomics.org/2008/10/five-ways-to-wellbeing-the-evidence (accessed 12 December 2019).

7 Be Prayerful

1 The Art of Examen, www.24-7prayer.com/theartofexamen (accessed 27 May 2020).
2 NIV UK 2011.
3 Psalm 46:10.
4 Based in the Lord's Prayer. See for example Matthew 6:9–13.
5 The wording used here for the Lord's Prayer is a mix of various versions simplified for use by all. This has been developed over time in our centres and is proving to be simple, memorable and yet accurate and true to the original Greek.
6 John 6:35.
7 www.ffald-y-brenin.org (accessed 16 May 2020).

8 Be in Partnership

1 An interview with Ruth Rice and Rachel Scott – March 2018. Used with permission.

[2] www.scie.org.uk (accessed 22 May 2020).
[3] https://www.inspireculture.org.uk/whats-on/news/2018/05/11/inspire-awards-results/ (accessed 1 June 2020).

9 Get Active

[1] The renew centre manual is available on www.renewwellbeing.org.uk/resources for churches that sign up to the process of setting up a centre and is offered here as part of the book. Edited for the purposes of this book.
[2] https://www.england.nhs.uk/mental-health/ (accessed 29 May 2020).
[3] www.renewwellbeing.org.uk/resources.

12 Forging Ahead

[1] https://www.eauk.org/church/research-and-statistics/how-many-churches-have-opened-or-closed-in-recent-years.cfm (accessed 28 May 2020). The Evangelical Alliance here use the work of Peter Brierley, *UK Church Statistics 2010–2020* (Tonbridge: ADBC Publishers, 2015).

Appendix 1

[1] Acts 17:28.
[2] Psalm 84:1.
[3] Psalm 72:19, paraphrase by author.
[4] Ephesians 2:22.
[5] 1 Corinthians 3:16.
[6] Galatians 2:20 (NLT).
[7] Acts 17:28.
[8] John 1:14.

Appendix 3

[1] www.freshstreams.net (accessed 26 May 2020).
[2] See Genesis 17:17; 18:12.

5 Ways to Inner Wellbeing

*Prayerful habits to help you
stay peaceful*

Ruth Rice

We all know that maintaining our mental health is becoming
increasingly important as our lives are under so many stresses and
strains, but we don't always know how to practically do that.

Ruth Rice shares simple steps that we can use to build new habits
into our daily lives. Based on the five ways of wellbeing (connect,
keep learning, get active, take notice and give), Ruth provides a
biblical and prayerful framework to help us see that God is interested
in our whole being: mind, body and soul.

Discover simple and sustainable inner ways to wellbeing.

Available as e-book only
978-1-78893-191-5

Infused with Life

*Exploring God's gift of rest in
a world of busyness*

Andy Percey

In a stressful, task-orientated life, we know the importance of rest,
but it is too often pushed out of our busy schedules.

Join Andy Percey as he reveals that rest is actually God's good gift to
us, provided for us to experience a balance in our lives that isn't just
about rest as recovery, but rest as harmony with our Creator and the
world he has made.

By learning to practise life-giving rhythms of rest, we can be infused
with the very best of the life God freely gives us.

978-1-78893-065-9

Ever Present

*Running to survive, thrive
and believe*

Austen Hardwick

Strokes, brain surgery, epilepsy . . . where is God in the middle of our suffering?

After surviving three strokes in his forties, Austen Hardwick began to think more deeply about life and faith. As he started to recover, he realised that running created space in which he could draw closer to God.

Weaving together personal testimony and biblical teaching, Austen encourages us to run towards God rather than away from him, so that we, too, can learn to live life in all its fullness with an ever-present God who is with us in our struggles.

Genuine, real and inspirational, *Ever Present* explores how running can be good for both the heart and the soul.

978-1-78893-136-6

Our Precious Lives

*Why telling and hearing stories
can save the church*

Steve Morris

In a world of increasing social fragmentation and loneliness,
Our Precious Lives demonstrates how listening to others can be
transformational in creating a sense of belonging. Inspiring stories
are grounded by practical ideas to put storytelling at the heart of the
church, and questions in each chapter encourage us all to glimpse
more of God, revel in our uniqueness and realize that we all have
something valuable to offer as his followers.

Underpinned by practical pastoral experience, this is a book full
of quirky and unexpected life stories that open us up afresh to the
beauty of life and our God.

978-1-78893-079-6

Finding Our Voice

*Unsung lives from the Bible
resonating with stories from today*

Jeannie Kendall

The Bible is full of stories of people facing issues that are still
surprisingly relevant today. Within its pages, people have wrestled
with problems such as living with depression, losing a child,
overcoming shame, and searching for meaning. Yet these are not
always the stories of the well-known heroes of faith, but those of
people whose names are not even recorded.

Jeannie Kendall brings these unnamed people to vibrant life. Their
experiences are then mirrored by a relevant testimony from someone
dealing with a similar situation today.

Finding Our Voice masterfully connects the past with the present day,
encouraging us to identify with the characters' stories, and giving us
hope that, whatever the circumstances, we are all 'known to God'.

978-1-78893-037-6

Salt Water and Honey

*Lost dreams, good grief,
and a better story*

Lizzie Lowrie

Reeling from the disappointment of a failed business venture, Lizzie Lowrie's life takes a nightmarish turn as she suffers miscarriage after miscarriage.

Written from the messy middle of life, where there are no neat or clichéd answers, Lizzie honestly shares her pain and the fight to find God in her suffering.

Providing a safe space to remind people that they're not alone, it's okay to grieve and their story matters, this is for anyone who has lost their dream and is struggling to understand their purpose when life looks nothing like they hoped it would.

978-1-78893-095-6

A Time to Hope

*365 Daily devotions from
Genesis to Revelation*

Naomi Reed

Many of us have favourite Bible verses that we draw comfort from, but we don't always know their context or understand how they fit into the main story arc of the Bible.

Tracing the big picture of God's story through the key themes and events from Genesis to Revelation allows us to see the abundant riches in God's Word. As you read the unfolding story day by day, you can encounter God in all his glorious holiness and faithfulness.

If you have ever struggled to read the Bible from cover to cover, then this devotional will help you find a way in to God's big story and help you fall in love with Jesus all over again.

978-1-78893-144-1

Authentic

We trust you enjoyed reading this book from Authentic. If you want to be informed of any new titles from this author and other releases you can sign up to the Authentic newsletter by scanning below:

Online:
authenticmedia.co.uk

Follow us: